WOMEN ENTREPRENEURS MASTER FINANCIAL SKILLS

Coletta J. Thomas

TABLE OF CONTENTS

ABSTRACT xiii

CHAPTER 1: INTRODUCTION TO THE STUDY 1

Study Background/Foundation 4

Current State of the Field in which the Problem Exists.................. 9

Historical Background.. 10

Deficiencies in the Evidence 11

Foundational Feminist Theory 12

Problem Statement.. 14

Audience 6

Specific Business Problem 7

Purpose of the Study 7

Methodology and Research Design Overview.. 8

Research Questions... 12

Study Limitations and Biases 13

Study Delimitations 15

Definitions of Key Terms 17

Summary... 18

CHAPTER 2: book REVIEW 20

Foundational Feminist Theories 22

Feminist Empiricism 25

Feminist Standpoint Theory 27

Poststructural Feminism 29

Entrepreneurship 31

Small Businesses 35

Microenterprise 36

Women Entrepreneurs 39

Characteristics of Women Entrepreneurs 41

Women Entrepreneur Industries..55

COVID-19 Pandemic Impact on Women Entrepreneurs 57

Financial Literacy 60

Financial Literacy Definitions...60

The Importance of Financial Literacy 61

Financial Literacy Importance for Entrepreneurship...................64

Financial Literacy Gender Gaps..65

Financial Literacy Measurements..66

Financial Literacy and Microenterprises 68

Fintech..70

Summary..72

CHAPTER 3: METHODOLOGY 74

Research Method 76

Research Design 78

Conceptual Framework 80

Data Collection..81

Audio Recording 84

Video Recording 85

Participants 88

Participant Search 88

Sampling Methodology 89

Recruitment of Participants 92

Sample Size 93

Data Analysis Methods 94

Organizing and Preparing the Data 95

Looking at the Data 95

Coding the Data 96

Developing Categories 97

Developing Themes 100

Interpretation of Themes 102

Limitations and Biases 103

Delimitations 105

Summary 106

CHAPTER 4: FINDINGS 108

Participant Selection and Demographics 110

Data Analysis Procedure 115

Presentation of Findings 117

Theme 1: Self-Sufficiency 119

Theme 2: Support Systems 122

Theme 3: Insignificant Skills and Strategies 127

Theme 4: SARS-CoV-2 Impact 131

Theme 5: Subject of Finance... 134

Theme 6: Sentiment of Passion 142

Summary... 144

CHAPTER 5: CONCLUSIONS AND DISCUSSION.............................. 148

Discussion of Findings and Conclusions 149

Research Question 1 150

Research Question 2 155

Research Question 3 163

Application of Findings and Conclusions to the Problem Statement 169

Application to Business 174

Recommendations for Action 177

Recommendations for Further Research.. 180

Concluding Statement.. 182

ABSTRACT

The lack of financial literacy programs for women entrepreneurs may result in their limited knowledge and understanding of financial skills. Three foundational research questions guided this study to (a) determine how women microentrepreneurs defined and used their financial literacy skills to run a tenable business; (b) explore how the women microentrepreneurs acquired these financial skills; and (c) identify financial approaches, strategies, and challenges faced by microentrepreneurs to better understand if they felt they were systemically oppressed from receiving equal treatment due to a lack of financial literacy skills. Through interviewing 22 women microentrepreneurs in the Pacific Northwest that had fewer than 5 employees, the problem was examined from a poststructural feminist lens and conducted using a qualitative methodology and phenomenological design. Data were collected through individual, semi-structured interviews, which were then transcribed and broken down into codes, categories, and themes and then turned into comprehensive findings that answered the foundational research questions. The audience of the study are current and future women entrepreneurs, policymakers, and institutions of higher education, who can affect gender equality, tenability of women microentrepreneurs, and the U.S. economy, positively. The goal of the study was to determine if financial literacy should be taught and measured differently for women entrepreneurs to combat existing gender gaps in financial literacy, and a key finding indicated the financial nomenclature that was used by the participants was different than what is found in academia and finance, which presented a deterrent in the participants acquiring additional financial skills. Another key finding of the study was participants were self-sufficient and passionate in their endeavors when they knew their

numbers and reviewed their finances often. Academia, policymakers, governmental entities, and entrepreneurs could use the results of this study to change the financial nomenclature that is commonly used and institute a language to teach financial literacy to different demographics, which can have a direct and positive impact on the financial literacy gender gap between men and women.

CHAPTER 1: INTRODUCTION TO THE STUDY

The purpose and primary focus of this study was to examine how women entrepreneurs used financial literacy skills to run a business and make decisions to determine if the strategies and skills employed helped or hindered their business goals. Exploring financial literacy from the women entrepreneur's perspective can provide data that could impact how and what is used to measure financial literacy for this specific group. Such information also can shed light on determining how financial literacy skills should be taught to women with entrepreneurial ambitions to combat existing gender gaps. Using a qualitative methodology and a phenomenological exploratory approach, the researcher conducted interviews with women entrepreneurs who owned a business for at least 5 years before, during, and post SARS-CoV-2, hereafter referred to as the COVID19, to explore how they used skills to navigate their businesses. For this study, before the pandemic means the business began in or before 2019 through March 14, 2020 (before), March 15, 2020, through May 31, 2021 (during) and June 1, 2021, and thereafter (postCOVID-19). These date parameters were chosen specifically to be in alignment with the mandated shutdowns of nonessential businesses and subsequent reopening procedures in states in the Pacific Northwest, with Washington state being the last state to reopen in Washington (Washington Governor Jay Inslee, 2021). The importance of capturing data from this period was to examine if there were any differences or similarities in the financial strategies and skills used during the COVID-19 pandemic.

Obtaining a clearer understanding of what financial literacy means to women entrepreneurs has the potential to reduce gender bias for women entrepreneurs.

Women entrepreneurship in the United States (U.S.) has been on the rise as the percentage of women business formations increased from 28% in 2019 to 49% in 2021 (Masterson, 2022). The U.S. Small Business Administration (SBA) reported that women entrepreneurs have impacted economic growth in the U.S., contributing $1.8 trillion to the economy and employing over 10 million workers in 2019 (SBA, 2023a). The economic conditions continued to improve in the U.S. into 2021, with $3.0 trillion in sales, representing 23 million workers (World Bank, n.d.). Despite the increase in women-owned businesses, gender gaps continued to exist in entrepreneurship. Businesses administered by male entrepreneurs have a higher survival rate, are approved for loans more often, receive more external funding, and are less impacted financially during a crisis (Fisher & Ryan, 2021; Lusardi et al., 2021; Milken Institute, 2021; World Bank, n.d.).

Although there are many factors associated with the rise in women's entrepreneurship and resulting contributions to the U.S. economy, one of the leading factors of women's entrepreneurship tenability is attributed to financial literacy, and the lack thereof is directly associated with entrepreneurship failure (Burchi et al., 2021; Nitani et al., 2020). To their detriment, women are considered less financially literate than men. This lack

of financial literacy places them at a disadvantage, because financially

literacy is correlated with better outcomes for wealth accumulation for

individuals (Lusardi, 2019), business growth, success, and a competitive

advantage for businesses (Anshika, 2022; Baporikar & Akino, 2020). Having

a competitive advantage is supported by the SBA (2024), which indicated

that competitiveness is a way for small businesses to gain an advantage over

others in the same industry; however, nationwide

assessments conducted by academics, profit, nonprofit, and government

institutions have indicated that women are less financially literate than men.

These assessments have been determined mainly through quantitative

measurements to assess individuals' knowledge of mortgage interest, bond

prices, compound interest, rates of return, and risk diversification (Fisher &

Ryan, 2021; Milken Institute, 2021; World Bank, n.d.). Other self-

assessments have confirmed these findings, including the Consumer

Financial Protection Bureau's (2020) financial empowerment test that bases

one's financial knowledge in three areas: (a) what one knows, (b) how what

one knows makes them feel, and finally (c) the experience level an individual

has with financial concepts (e.g., having a savings account or credit card).

The Consumer Financial Protection Bureau (n.d.) also published a glossary of

terms to aid in financial nomenclature, which could be used to prepare

anyone taking the self-assessment. Although knowledge in these areas is

valuable to better understand the status of financial literacy at the individual

level, the questions asked on standardized financial literacy tests do not address financial decisions critical to starting, growing, and maintaining a business. Therefore, the lower rates of financial literacy skills between men and women entrepreneurs can potentially diminish the economic growth that women entrepreneurs contribute to the U.S. economy.

Discounting the events of the COVID-19 pandemic, beginning in 2020 when the world faced a setback that no one had ever witnessed before, would be negligent. During this time, business closures forced certain entities to shut down permanently or temporarily (Centers for Disease Control and Prevention [CDC], 2020). Specific to small businesses, closures outpaced business formations in the first 6 months of 2020 (Wilmoth, 2021). Additionally, Wilmoth (2021) found although recovery efforts ensued, data have indicated that women-owned businesses were impacted more than men-owned businesses, facing a decline of 22.1% versus 19.1%, respectively. As this current research looked at women-owned companies who had been in business for at least 5 years, the anomaly of 2020 makes understanding the financial strategies and skills that potentially aided in financial decisions used by women entrepreneurs to navigate the pandemic even more important.

Study Background/Foundation

Financial literacy has become an important topic and while women entrepreneurs have significantly impacted economic growth, there continues to be gender gaps in entrepreneurship as it relates to financial literacy (Fisher & Ryan, 2021; Lusardi et al., 2021; Milken Institute, 2021; World Bank, n.d.). Financial literacy is considered a necessary resource to any organization through various stages of business, and it has been found that women entrepreneurs are negatively impacted by financial internal and external constraints (Baporikar & Akino, 2020; Carranza et al., 2018). Internally, research has suggested that more training opportunities should be available to women entrepreneurs to assist with education on debt and how to recognize financial opportunities from different sectors (Carranza et al., 2018). However, contrary to research by Carranza et al. (2018), Abdul Latif Jameel Poverty Action Lab (2023) conducted a review of 28 randomized training programs for microenterprises and concluded that courses offered to microentrepreneurs had only modest impacts on key business outcomes. Externally, women entrepreneurs are outpaced by men in obtaining SBA loans and denied external funding at a rate of 25%, which is greater than men entrepreneurs at 19% (U.S. Senate Committee on Small Business & Entrepreneurship, 2023). It has also been found that women entrepreneurs receive less funding from venture capitalists and these statistics worsened from 2.4% in 2021 to 1.9% in 2022 (D. Davis, 2023). Figure 1.1 represents the percentage of venture capital that went to women-only founders and women and men cofounders. Figure 1.1 highlights that the trend of coownership with a man involved in obtaining venture capital has been growing for coowned businesses compared to women-owned businesses (Pitchbook, 2024). The latest data through December 31, 2023, have shown women-owned businesses received 2.0%, and co-owned businesses received 20.7%.

Figure 1.1

Women (CO-) Founded VC Capital %

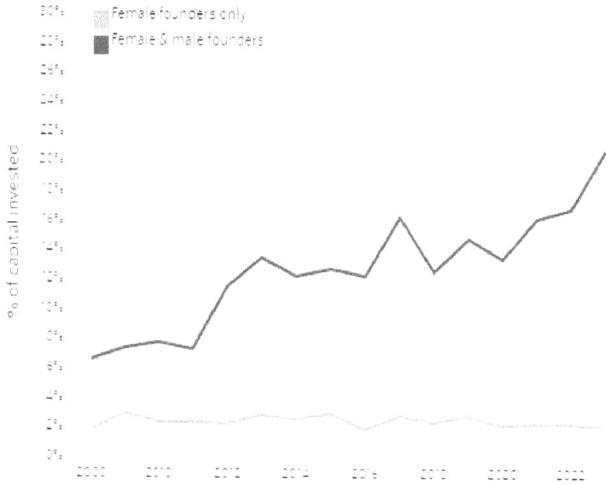

Note. This figure is a replication from Pitchbook (2024), a data source platform that supplies data on start-up companies and mergers and acquisitions.

This study looked to women entrepreneurs who have small businesses, and the book review in Chapter 2 discusses how the terms "entrepreneurship" and "small business" have been used interchangeably and how the definition of entrepreneurship has evolved. This study used the term microenterprises to represent the small businesses owned by women entrepreneurs.

Financial literacy is defined in many ways by policy makers, government institutions, organizations, and scholars. The Organization for Economic Cooperation and Development (OECD, 2023) defined financial literacy as having awareness, knowledge, skills, and behaviors to make financial decisions to achieve individual well-being and has been supported by the *Big Five* financial literacy assessment (Global Financial Literary Excellence Center, n.d.). Similarly, a research report written by Cooper (2021), commissioned by the Congressional Research Center, added that knowledge of the "tools that equip people to make individual financial decisions and take action to attain their goals" (p. 3) as another layer of financial literacy. The Corporate Finance Institute (n.d.) defined financial literacy in more specific terms such as knowing about budgeting, taxation, and investing. Like the individual, financial literacy has its benefits to an entrepreneur. Research has shown that financially literate entrepreneurs can manage their businesses more proficiently (Anshika, 2022), minimize financial risks (Vidovicova, 2021), and evolve into better chances of success (Usama & Wan Yusoff, 2018). Although there are many definitions and uses of financial literacy, the common themes in these definitions are knowledge, behaviors, abilities, and action. OECD (2023) articulated the specific skills that are deemed vital for women entrepreneurs to have to start, operate, and grow a business.

The OECD (2022) and its International Network on Financial Education established a framework for the core competencies of which small businesses should have knowledge and included choice and use of financial services, financial and business management planning, risk and insurance, and financial landscape. Under each core competency, the information is further broken down by specific skills and behaviors one should have to own a business (OECD, 2022). The framework report by the OECD includes recommended skills such as revenue tracking, payments and deposits, inventory, cash flow, preparation of financial documents, and budgeting.

Another skill that has been identified as an essential for entrepreneurship through a systematic book review is financial forecasting (Mamabola & Myres, 2020). Financial forecasting is defined as the process of looking at historical data to project what may happen in the future (Boyles, 2022), and four common methodologies are used: (a) straight-line, (b) moving average, (c) simple linear regression, and (d) multiple linear regression. In addition to using historical data to forecast future sales or revenues, another form of forecasting is using variability analysis, which entails looking backward at data points to arrive at averages to predict future earnings (Scott, 2020). Furthermore, Chandi (2024) found that forecasting has many benefits to small businesses, including being better prepared for dealing with times of unpredictability and aiding in the growth and resilience of a business. However, contrary to financial forecasting being essential for small businesses, other research has shown that financial forecasting has been linked to making poor decisions, as it sets a reference point for the business owner; when that reference point is not met, it leads to riskier decision making (Shrader et al., 2021).

There are some other noteworthy programs, including the SBA (2023k), which implemented a program entitled, Money Smart for Small Business. This program has an online toolkit to help small businesses learn about specific financial literacy skills including earning, spending, and borrowing (SBA, 2023k). Another program specifically for women

entrepreneurs is the DreamBuilder (2018) program, which provides courses

on what to include in a business plan; understanding value; setting prices;

profit, loss, and break-even analysis; financial statements analysis; accounts

receivables and payables; bookkeeping; cash flow; and projections. Goldman

Sachs (2023) also created an online educational program for women

entrepreneurs and included modules on business finance that cover financial

statement analysis, assets and liabilities, ratio analysis, and financial

terminology. According to the Institute of Entrepreneurship Development,

the financial skills women entrepreneurs should possess are identical to that

of the DreamBuilder courses and adds skills on return on investment and

taxation (Bouronikos, 2022). Because a lack of financial literacy skills has

been considered one of the leading factors in women entrepreneurship failure

(Burchi et al., 2021; Nitani et al., 2020), these programs were designed to

educate for better chances of empowerment and success for women

entrepreneurs.

Current State of the Field in which the Problem Exists

Researchers and policymakers alike have recognized the gender gap in

entrepreneurship as an ongoing issue in the U.S. To continue to bolster

women entrepreneurs' involvement, the United States Patent and Trademark

Office (USPTO, 2022) in conjunction with the U.S. Department of Congress

in November 2022, launched a new program to increase women's

participation in the economy through an initiative titled Women's

Entrepreneurship. The goal of Women's Entrepreneurship is to assist women entrepreneurs with information about starting a business, guidance on protecting intellectual property, securing funding, and networking with other women entrepreneurs to continually promote the economic contribution that women entrepreneurship brings to the U.S. economy (USPTO, 2022). The Women's Entrepreneurship launch followed a proclamation by President Biden, which named November 2022 as the first-ever National Entrepreneurship Month and November 19 as Women's Entrepreneurship Day (USPTO, 2022). Women's Entrepreneurship and the Biden administration's proclamation supported the notion that gender gaps in entrepreneurship exist and are of concern for the U.S. government. According to the joint press release, men are owners in approximately 80% of U.S. businesses and own a majority of shares in 63% of those businesses, compared to 37% of women-owned businesses, with only 21% owning a majority of shares (USPTO, 2022). These efforts serve as another example of resources being applied to repair the gender gaps experienced by women entrepreneurs.

Historical Background

Although women were active in entrepreneurship before the 20th century, there was little to no academic book published to differentiate the phenomenon of entrepreneurship between men and women. In her groundbreaking work, Schwartz (1976) published the first journal article on women entrepreneurship entitled *Entrepreneurship: A New Female Frontier*. In the study, Schwartz conducted a qualitative study using 20 women-owned companies to explore the traits, motivations, and personal attitudes of women entrepreneurs' needs for success, independence, economic reward, and work satisfaction. Almost 20 years later, the first book written on women entrepreneurship was published by Goffee and Scase (1985). In these earlier publications, researchers believed there was no specific need for a separate investigation of men and women entrepreneurs because it was assumed they were the same (Yadav & Unni, 2016). It was not until 2009 that a niche journal on the study of women entrepreneurs was established, which prompted the need to examine men and women entrepreneurship as two different entities (Brush et al., 2009). Since that time, book has expanded, with results showing there are still gender gaps in the field of entrepreneurship (Yadav & Unni, 2016).

The passing of the Women's Business Ownership Act (1988) and development of various programs by the SBA (2021b) demonstrated a historical pattern of efforts made by the U.S. government to promote women entrepreneurship. Furthermore, publications of academic book, books, and reports added to the historical development of the recognition of women entrepreneurship as its own phenomenon. Additional details can be found in Chapter 2, book Review.

Deficiencies in the Evidence

Since the late 1970s, women entrepreneurship gaps have been explored through various lenses, such as motivational (Robichaud et al., 2019), personality (Zisser et al., 2019), and success factors (Welsh et al., 2021). Based on these findings, researchers have claimed the inequalities are based on gender stereotypes, roles, and expectations, which have caused negative

repercussions to women entrepreneurs and more exploration into what is

needed to "level the gendered playing field" (Fisher & Ryan, 2021, p. 243).

Scholars also have requested the field of women entrepreneurship branch out

to examine the financial literacy deficiencies women entrepreneurs

experience, specifically through a feminist lens (Ahl & Marlow, 2012; Foss

et al., 2019; Wigginton & Lafrance, 2019).

Furthermore, a bibliometric analysis of over 2,800 articles conducted by

Cardella et al. (2020) concluded that the least explored area of women

entrepreneurs is an examination of the topic from a feminist lens viewpoint.

Goyal and Kumar (2021) identified a need to dig deeper into the *why* the

gender gap exists in financial literacy because the *what* is oversaturated.

Although finding answers to *why* the gender gap exists in financial literacy

may be true from the perspective of Goyal and Kumar (2021), the focus of

this study was on w*hat* and *how* questions to better understand the topic of

women entrepreneurs and the importance of financial literacy skills through a

poststructural feminist lens.

Foundational Feminist Theory

Poststructural feminist theory posits that acts of discrimination between

men and women is not sex-based but a result of the social construct, which

changes over time (Foss et al., 2019; Lather, 1992). Previous research on

women entrepreneurship has had a massive impact on comparative analyses

to suggest how women can be *fixed* to adapt to the male-dominated sphere of entrepreneurship either through training or policies (Ahl & Nelson, 2015;

Foss et al., 2019). There has been a desire to investigate women

entrepreneurship deficiencies in a different manner, which has resulted in

defining women entrepreneurship from the women's perspective to get rid of

the presumptions and define women entrepreneurship through their lived

experiences (Ahl & Marlow, 2012). Using the framework of exploring

definitions through the lens of the knower can provide different perspectives

on what constitutes a deficiency in the financial literacy skills of women

entrepreneurs versus what is essential for them to know.

Researchers have studied the topic using feminist empiricism, feminist

standpoint theory, and poststructural feminism; with each lens, different

perspectives relate to diverse ways of defining gender equality, problem

constructions, and policy change suggestions (Foss et al., 2019; Wigginton &

Lafrance, 2019). There are many shapes and forms of feminist theory, as

indicated by the founder of feminist theory, Mary

Wollstonecraft (1792/2004), in the late 1700s and feminist theory has gone

through many stages to progress equal rights for women (Mohajan, 2022).

Mohajan (2022) produced a comprehensive paper outlining the four stages of

feminism beginning with the first stage (i.e., 1800s through the 1920s), which

brought about political equality for women and the right to vote. Mohajan

outlined the second stage (i.e., 1963 through the 1990s) as a time that brought

about economic equality through the Equal Pay Act and addressed education,

sexuality, and reproductive rights through various legislations. Mohajan

described the third stage of feminism (i.e., 1991 through the 2000s) as a focus on equal rights for women, including inclusivity regardless of sexuality, race, class, and gender. Finally, Mohajan described the fourth stage (i.e., 2012 to current) as a time defined by technology whereby social media has acted as the vehicle for spreading the word of equality.

Overall, feminist theory seeks to address women's societal, political, and legal inequalities. At each stage, a variety of feminist movements have emerged, all with the goal of achieving equality for women. Although various lenses of feminist theory exist, this study focused on poststructural feminist theory, which aims to understand the inequalities from the perspective of the women entrepreneur.

Problem Statement

The general problem is that women in the U.S. have been considered less financially literate based on quantitative results, which have perpetuated inequalities in entrepreneurship such as external access to funding, loan disapprovals, and survival rates (Fisher & Ryan, 2021; Lusardi et al., 2021; Milken Institute, 2021; World Bank, n.d.). Closing these gender gaps could result in a 3% to 6% growth in gross domestic product in the U.S. (U.S. Senate Committee on Small Business & Entrepreneurship, 2023). The gender gaps were exemplified based on data from the Board of Governors of the Federal Reserve System, as reported by Tranfaglia et al. (2024). The results of the financial literacy gap were taken from the 2021 Survey of Household Economics and Decision Making (SHED), which was a survey that was based on three questions, including interest, inflation, and diversification. The survey had a total of 100 questions, and the results indicated that men exceeded in answering questions correctly and women exceeded men in

answering incorrectly and responding, "Don't Know." Figure 1.2 is a visual

representation of the results from the survey.

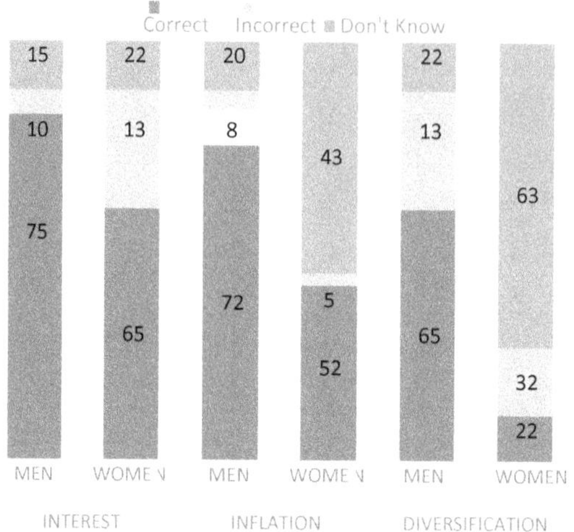

Note. This is a replication of the results of the findings reported by Tranfaglia et al.

(2024) based on results from the 2021 SHED report.

Furthermore, the U.S. government has spent billions of dollars in resources for women entrepreneurs (Bitti, 2021), yet gender gaps continue to exist. The financial literacy results have been substantiated based on nationwide assessments conducted by academics, profit, nonprofit, and government institutions (Fisher & Ryan, 2021; Lusardi & Mitchell, 2014; Milken Institute, 2021; U.S. Financial Literacy and Education Commission, 2020; World Bank, n.d.). In a report authored by Urban and Valdes (2022) through the Financial Industry Regulatory Authority Investor Education Foundation, there has been a decline in financial literacy levels year over year

Figure

since 2009 through 2021. Figure 1.3 displays the downward trend in financial

literacy skills from 2009 through 2021, based on the results published by

Urban and Valdes (2022) through the FINRA Investor Education Foundation,

which has published financial literacy data on the U.S. since 2009, every 3

years.

1.3

*Trends in Overall Financial Literacy From 2009 Through 2021 Correct
Responses*

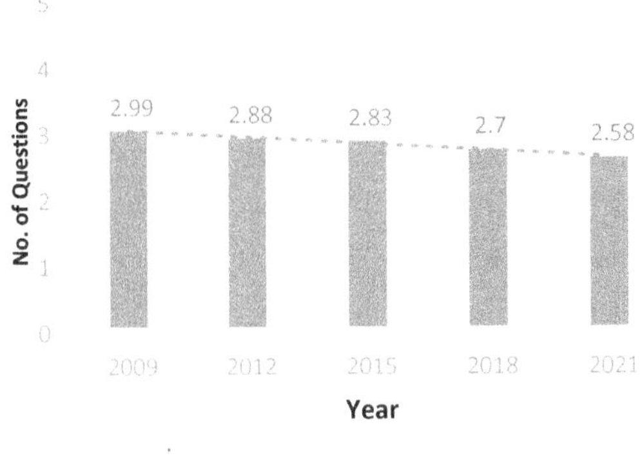

Note. The data displays that in 2009, respondents were able to answer 3
questions out of

5 correctly, compared to 2.6 out of 5 in 2021, a 14% drop.

Figure 1.4 displays the downward trend in financial literacy skills from

2009 through 2021, based on the results published by Urban and Valdes

(2022) through the

FINRA Investor Education Foundation, based on "Don't Know" responses.

1.4

Figure

Trends in Overall Financial Literacy From 2009 Through 2021 "Don't Know"

Responses

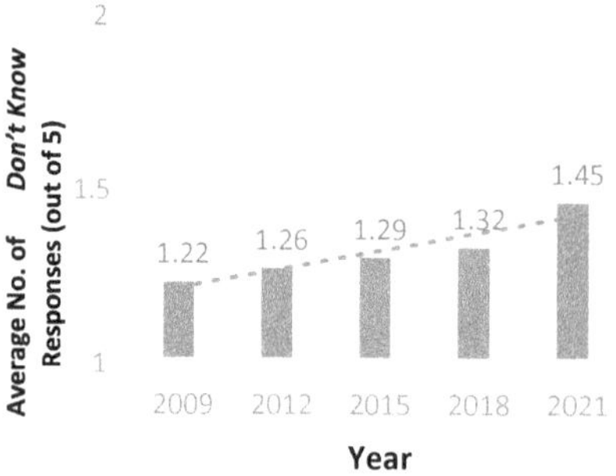

Note. Based on thes same survey conducted by Urban and Valdes (2022),

Figure 1.4 displays the increase in "Don't Know" responses, using the same

set of 5 questions.

In these results, women fared worse than men in responding correctly;

15% versus 26%, respectively, and "Don't Know" responses were also higher

for women.

Figure 1.5 is a graphical depiction of the correct and "Don't Know"
responses by gender.

1.5

Changes in Average Number of Correct and "Don't Know" Responses From 2009

Through 2021 by Gender

Figure

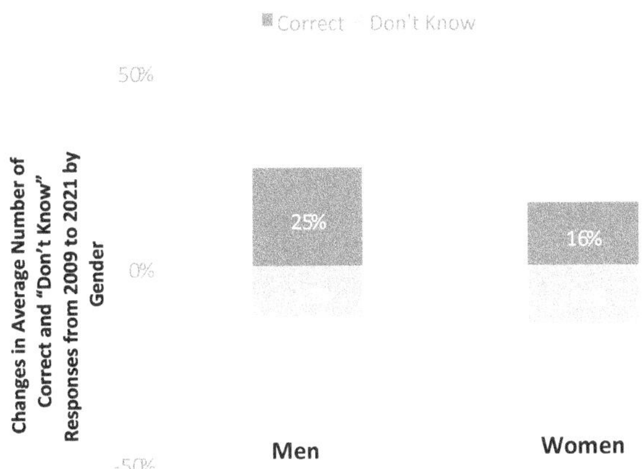

Note. This is a recreation of a figure from the report by Urban and Valdes (2022).

However, the questions that Urban and Valdes (2022) asked were geared toward individual financial literacy, such as knowledge on mortgage interest, bond prices, compound interest, rates of return, and risk diversification, not entrepreneurs. Local programs that are geared specifically for entrepreneurs, such as the Washington Women's Business Center (2023), have claimed that they has served over 1,309 clients. However, the Washington Women's Business Center does not state specifically how the clients have been served because they offer a variety of support for business skills, training, and coaching. The gender gap problems for entrepreneurs have also been recognized by the U.S. Senate Committee on Small Business and Entrepreneurship (2023) by calling for the expansion of federal programs for women entrepreneurs.

Audience

This qualitative study was performed to contribute to the existing book on the knowledge of business practices of women entrepreneurs through a feminist lens. The research can benefit women entrepreneurs, policymakers, and institutions of higher education, positively impacting gender equality, tenability, society, and the U.S. economy. Women entrepreneurship can benefit from this study from findings that can result in improved financial performance and tenability, which can positively impact society, the economy, and gender equality.

The research can also benefit policymakers by providing critical information on the tools deemed essential to women entrepreneurship tenability. The knowledge gained can lead to changes in existing programs and the development of innovative programs. The research can also contribute to a more comprehensive definition of financial literacy, leading to positive social changes, accelerating economic growth, and addressing gender gaps in entrepreneurship.

Lastly, the research can benefit institutions of higher education in curriculum development to ensure the topics deemed essential to women entrepreneurs are offered and addressed. Enhanced and innovative curriculums can lead to better results in the tenability of women entrepreneurship. Benefits to academics can also include new insights on women entrepreneurship to address gender inequality issues from the poststructural feminist view.

Specific Business Problem

The specific problem is the lack of financial literacy programs for entrepreneurs may result in limited knowledge and understanding of financial skills used by womenowned businesses in the Pacific Northwest and how those skills are obtained.

Understanding the needs of women microentrepreneurs in the Pacific Northwest area can have a significant impact on the tenability of their businesses, adding to the discourse on their economic activities.

Purpose of the Study

The purpose of this qualitative study was to explore the meaning, knowledge, and use of financial literacy skills of women entrepreneurs who owned and operated a microenterprise in the Pacific Northwest in the U.S. before, during, and post COVID-19 from a feminist lens. Therefore, the research contributed to the gap in the book by examining how women entrepreneurs defined and used their financial literacy skills to run a tenable business and to better understand if they felt they were systemically oppressed from receiving equal treatment due to a lack in financial literacy skills. Using a qualitative methodology and phenomenological approach, interviews were conducted to better understand the lived experiences of those being researched (Creswell & Creswell, 2018).

Methodology and Research Design Overview

The following section summarizes the methodology and research design that were used to conduct research on women entrepreneurship and financial literacy to contribute to existing book on the topic. A more detailed discussion of the methodology and research can be found in Chapter 3. The research used the qualitative methodology and a phenomenological research design to explore the lives of women entrepreneurs and the financial strategies used to run a tenable business.

Due to the oversaturation of existing quantitative results on women entrepreneurs and financial literacy skills, which all indicated women entrepreneurs are less financially literate than men (Lusardi et al., 2021; Nicolini & Haupt, 2019; Skagerlund et al., 2018), the current study explored the financial literacy skills used by women entrepreneurs through a qualitative methodology. Using the qualitative method enables researchers to explore phenomena in their natural setting using interviews with participants (Creswell & Creswell, 2018). Using the qualitative methodology enables researchers to collect data through multiple sources, such as interviews and observations, which depict the participants' own words.

The target population for this study was women microentrepreneurs who owned and operated a microenterprise in the Pacific Northwest. There are varying definitions of a small business. The U.S. Bureau of Labor Statistics (2018) defined an establishment with less than 100 employees as a small business. The SBA (2023j) defined a small business based on three criteria: (a) industry, (b) sales receipts, and (c) number of employees.

Industry and sales receipts vary; however, the number of employees is

typically met by 500 or less, including businesses that operate with one or no

employees

(SBA, 2023j). The OECD (2023) defined a small business as an enterprise with less than

250 employees and continued to subdivide businesses and label enterprises

with less than 10 employees as a microenterprise. Research has also

deciphered small business in terms of micro and macro businesses, whereby

"micro" describes a business as its individual function and "macro" pertains

to clusters, or industry (Gianiodis et al., 2022). For example, the Washington

State Microenterprise Association (n.d.) defined a microenterprise as a

business consisting of 1 to 5 employees, including the business owner.

Legislation that amended the Small Business Act recognized a business with

less than 5 employees as a microenterprise (Microloan Amendments and

Modernization Act, 2007). Therefore, for the purpose of this study, and

because a certain industry was not the focus, a small business was defined at

the micro level and included businesses with less than 5 employees. The

Pacific Northwest includes the states of Idaho, Oregon, Washington, and

Montana, as declared by the Pacific Northwest Electric Power Planning and

Conservation Act (1980). The timeframe for study was before, during, and

post

COVID-19, through a feminist lens.

Most scholars recommend in-depth interviews of 5 to 25 participants (Dworkin, 2012; Marshall & Rossman, 2016). Therefore, the study used purposeful sampling in that the researcher sought out women microentrepreneurs, an effort that resulted in 22 participants, which exceeded the target of at least 20 businesses in the Pacific Northwest that had been in business before the COVID-19 pandemic beginning in or previous to 2019 to March 14, 2020 (before), March 15, 2020 to May 31, 2021 (during), and June, 2021 and thereafter (post COVID-19), and thereafter, which is when the last states in the Pacific Northwest were officially reopened (Washington Governor Jay Inslee, 2021), and had less than 5 employees. The women interviewed in this study had owned businesses with fewer than 5 employees, and obtaining the participant pool was done in various ways. First, the SBA (2023h) produces fact sheets on business ownership by state. According to the state fact sheets (SBA, 2023h) on Idaho, Montana, Oregon, and Washington state, there were 450,000 combined firms owned by women without employees and an additional 63,655 combined firms with employees for these four states at the time of the study. The fact sheets (SBA, 2023h) are developed from two U.S. Census Bureau databases: (a) Nonemployee Statistics by Demographics (NES-D), and (b) the Annual Business Survey (ABS). Using these fact sheets provided useful estimates for the potential population for this study but presented some issues. By combining the two databases, the years were different in that the NES-D data were from 2019, and the ABS data were from 2021. The fact sheets produced by the SBA (2023h) also did not differentiate businesses with employees by firm size, and because this study's

focus was on women microenterprises, which are businesses that have less

than 5 employees, the number of the potential population was overstated for

the study. Additionally, the 450,000 non-employee businesses notated on the

SBA (2023h) fact sheets included gig workers, contractors, and freelancers.

These groups are mostly businesses that are secondary and supplemental

sources of income that are filed using a 1099 form through the Internal

Revenue Service (Collins et al., 2019). Therefore, to provide a more accurate

population estimate, data were only pulled from the U.S. Census

Bureau ABS Survey and were filtered on the following criteria: (a)

geographical location (i.e., Idaho, Montana, Oregon, Washington), (b)

women, (c) 1 to 4 employees and 0 employees (National Center for Science

and Engineering Statistics within the National Science Foundation, & the

U.S. Census Bureau, 2021). The results of this database query of the ABS

data resulted in the following estimate of the number of participants in the

population for this study. Table 1.1 provides the breakdown of women-owned

businesses by state. The total population for this study was 46,268 businesses.

Table 1.1

*Women-Owned Businesses in the Pacific Northwest by State With 0
Employees and Less Than 5 Employees*

State	0 employees	1 to 4 employees	Total
Idaho	1,492	3,856	5,348
Montana	1,028	3,904	4,932
Oregon	3,063	10,814	13,877
Washington	4,907	17,204	22,111

| Total | 10,490 | 35,778 | 46,268 |

Note. The data was pulled from the National Center for Science and Engineering

Statistics within the National Science Foundation and U.S. Census Bureau (2021),

The data obtained were analyzed using the hierarchical approach used in qualitative research, which entails preparing the raw data to be analyzed, followed by transcribing, reading, coding, theming, and then interpreting the data into comprehensive findings (Creswell & Creswell, 2018). The methodology was akin to the Gadamerian hermeneutic phenomenology analytical framework as described by Alsaigh and Coyne (2021), which is a six-stage approach and includes (a) immersion, (b) understanding, (c) abstraction, (d) synthesis and theme development, (e) illumination and illustration of phenomena, and (f) integration and critique.

Research Questions

This qualitative phenomenological study explored the meaning, knowledge, and use of financial literacy skills of women microentrepreneurs who owned and operated a business in the Pacific Northwest. The timeframe under study were businesses that were operational for a total of 5 or more years, beginning in or previous to 2019 to March 14, 2020 (before), March 15, 2020 to May 31, 2021 (during), and June, 2021 and thereafter (post COVID-19) to gain insight on the differences or similarities in financial strategies and skills during the pandemic, because research had indicated that there were gender gaps in entrepreneurship during a crisis (Wilmoth, 2021).

The following research questions (RQs) aimed to better understand women entrepreneurs' financial skills and strategies used to run their businesses:

RQ1: What are women entrepreneurs' perceptions of the impact on their business through the lens of their current financial literacy?

RQ2: How do women entrepreneurs acquire the financial skills used in their business?

RQ3: What are the financial approaches, strategies, and challenges, if any, faced by women entrepreneurs?

Study Limitations and Biases

The limitations associated with the chosen research design included constraints typically found in research such as statistical model constraints, funding constraints, or other factors, including imposed restrictions (Theofanidis & Fountouki, 2019). The study took on a qualitative approach using interviews that were audio recorded and, for some interviews, video recorded. A limitation to this approach is that when participants are engaged in an audio-recorded interview, it can sometimes cause them to be unengaged and dishonest (McMullin, 2023). To overcome this hurdle, the researcher conducted preliminary discussions with participants to advise them that the interview would be recorded and not used outside the research to allay their anxiety. Furthermore, face-toface interviews can sometimes cause the

Hawthorne Effect, whereby participants alter their responses to appease the interviewer (BK et al., 2019). To overcome this limitation, building a rapport with participants is highly encouraged, which can be done by engaging in multiple conversations, stating the purpose of the study, and ensuring participants that there are no wrong or right responses; the researcher followed these parameters.

Video conferencing and recording can also cause limitations because participants may fear the data could end up online due to hacking, may be selfconscious of being videotaped, may be unfamiliar with the technology, and may not want to share openly during a conversation due to being unfamiliar with the interviewer (Van Zeeland et al., 2021). To overcome these obstacles, the researcher used bracketing, which requires setting aside any predispositions, thoughts, and beliefs to avoid bias in interviewing (Weatherford & Maitra, 2019). There was also engagement with the participants over several occurrences to help familiarize themselves with the technology and build a relationship for comfort.

Financial literacy can be viewed as a topic in which women may not wish to engage because, quantitatively, they are less financially literate than men (Nicolini & Haupt, 2019), which risks the potential of many not wanting to participate. To mitigate this challenge, the researcher engaged with participants through an invitation to clearly articulate the study's objective and indicated there were no preconceived notions by the researcher and it would not entail any quantitative measures. This approach was employed to help alleviate the fear of numbers often found in book (Apostolidu & Johnston-Wilder, 2023; Hasler et al., 2021).

Because the researcher identified with the participants to some extent, such as being women, a former entrepreneur, and having a background in finance, it was necessary to develop a plan to mitigate any biases. To do so, the researcher employed epoch, which is the process of looking at the phenomenon under study as newfound knowledge, void of any prejudgments and preconceptions (Moustakas, 1994). There are various ways epoch can be achieved, including bracketing, which is the process of suspending one's own beliefs and assumptions (Weatherford & Maitra, 2019). Epoch was achieved in this study by maintaining a reflexive journal, which can increase the rigor of the study. Additionally, dependability and confirmability rely on an audit trail maintained by the researcher to capture every step of the study, including a rationale for the study, methodological choice, elements of data collection, and analysis. Transferability was attained through providing rich, detailed, and accurate descriptions of the participants to enable future and current entrepreneurs to use the study results in their own business practices.

Study Delimitations

The study had delimitations that may render the findings not transferable to a broader population. There was a geographical delimitation because the participants' business locations were limited to the Pacific Northwest. The area was chosen for the diversity of a geographical region rather than focusing on one state and did not reflect the general population of women entrepreneurs throughout the U.S.

The qualitative methodology and phenomenological research design were also intentionally selected for the study because there is an abundance of book, quantitatively, on women entrepreneurs and financial literacy. Because a specific group of entrepreneurs were not interviewed in any specific industry, the study used an existing theory, and the phenomenological approach was selected as the research design because it seeks to better understand the lived experiences of the phenomenon under study.

The selection of women entrepreneurs was chosen deliberately because data have indicated repeatedly that women are less financially literate than men and the research intended to seek out why, from the women's' perspective. Furthermore, there was a delimitation on the population size of the business because the researcher sought out women microentrepreneurs, thereby excluding any women-owned companies that have 5 or more employees.

Finally, the study had intentional date parameters defined of an operational business, which was from 2019 and thereafter. During this time, the world went through a pandemic, and many companies were forced to shut down. Therefore, some findings may not be transferable to other future periods. These parameters were set intentionally to explore women entrepreneurship and the financial strategies utilized to endure a business during a pandemic.

Definitions of Key Terms

The following definitions were used throughout the study, and this section aimed to provide clarification to the readers on terms that may not be commonly known.

Entrepreneurship. Entrepreneurship is the process by which an individual or group owns a company that brings a new opportunity or process to the market or takes an existing business and makes substantial improvements to products, services, and processes (Center for American Entrepreneurship, n.d.).

Financial literacy. Being financially literate means having awareness, knowledge, skills, and behaviors to make financial decisions to achieve individual well-being (OECD, 2023).

Fintech. Fintech are tools that use apps, software, or technology that enable businesses and consumers to digitally manage their finances to gain insights and conduct transactions (Trificana, 2023).

Gender gap. The gender gap refers to systemic differences between men and women in the outcomes of attainments and attitudes on social, political, intellectual, cultural, and economic outcomes (Harris, 2017).

Microenterprise. This study used the term microenterprise to represent small businesses. A business operating under a sole proprietorship, partnership, or corporation that has fewer than 5 employees is defined as a microenterprise (Microloan Amendments and Modernization Act, 2007).

Microentrepreneur. A microentrepreneur is the owner or developer of a microenterprise (Microloan Amendments and Modernization Act, 2007).

Nonessential business. A nonessential business is one that does not supply operations and services to an industry that is essential to the continuity of critical functions in the U.S. (CDC, 2021).

Post COVID-19. In this study, post COVID-19 refers to the reopening of all businesses in Washington state, which occurred on June 30, 2021 (Washington Governor

Jay Inslee, 2021).

Tenable business. A tenable business is one that has been operational for at least 5 or more years, beginning in or before 2019 to March 14, 2020 (before); March 15, 2020, to May 31, 2021 (during); and June 1, 2021, and thereafter (post COVID-19).

Summary

The purpose of this qualitative study was to explore the problem of gender gaps in financial literacy in entrepreneurship by researching the lived experiences of 22 women microentrepreneurs in the Pacific Northwest through a feminist lens. In doing so, the study aimed to contribute to the gap in the book by examining how women microentrepreneurs defined and used their financial literacy skills to run a tenable business and explored if they felt they were systemically oppressed from perceived deficiencies such as stereotyping, roles, and expectations. The study also used a specific

timeframe to include companies that had been in business before, during, and

post COVID-19, as the pandemic negatively affected women entrepreneurs

more than men entrepreneurs, to learn if financial strategies and skills took on

a new meaning during this timeframe.

Research has indicated that women lack skills in financial literacy;

however, the results have been mostly based on quantitative studies and have

typically examined the topic from an individualistic perspective. Therefore,

the study used a qualitative and heuristic phenomenological approach,

whereby one-on-one interviews were used to deduce the participants' words

into rich and thick meanings that developed into a thematic formulation. The

researcher made all efforts to ensure participants were protected, and the

study was performed ethically to ensure trustworthiness. The findings of this

study can benefit existing and future women entrepreneurs, policymakers,

and academics by revealing what financial literacy means to women

entrepreneurs from their perspective. Although this introduction provides a

snapshot of the study, Chapter 2 delves deeper into the book to fully examine

the foundational theory of poststructural feminism, women entrepreneurship,

microentrepreneurs, and

financial literacy.

The purpose of this qualitative study was to explore the meaning, knowledge, and use of financial literacy skills of women entrepreneurs who owned and operated a microenterprise in the Pacific Northwest in the U.S. before, during, and post COVID-19 from a feminist lens. The research was intended to contribute to the gap in the book by examining how women entrepreneurs defined and used their financial literacy skills to run a tenable business and to better understand if they felt they were systemically oppressed from receiving equal treatment due to a lack in financial literacy skills. As such, this book review explored women entrepreneurship and financial literacy to better inform policymakers, women entrepreneurs, and academics on what the book says.

Women have come a very long way throughout the history of the U.S. They began as secondary citizens with the unattainability to vote or work outside of the home into growing into one of the largest phenomena in the nation's history, entrepreneurs (Cardella et al., 2020). Many debates exist on the definition of an entrepreneur, which still portrays women as inferior to men, whereby the masculine discourse in entrepreneurship is taken for granted as being normative (Ahl & Marlow, 2021). It was not until 1988 that women, nationally, could secure funding for a venture without a man as a cosigner (Wolfe, 2018). Historically, entrepreneurs have been associated with masculine attributes such as risk taking, and entrepreneurship follows in the same maledominated realm whereby commercial and social entrepreneurship have been correlated positively with perceptions of masculinity (Gupta et al.,

2022). These perceptions generally have been guided by societal norms;

however, despite the hurdles women have endured since the inception of the

U.S., more than ever, women entrepreneurs are making historical strides,

with there being over 12 million women entrepreneurs as of 2023 (U.S.

Senate Committee on Small Business & Entrepreneurship, 2023).

One of the leading factors of entrepreneurial success is the knowledge

of financial concepts to make better decisions to run a tenable business and

without this knowledge, there is a direct link associated with entrepreneurship

failure (Burchi et al., 2021; Nitani et al., 2020). Small businesses have always

had high failure rates, according to the U.S. Bureau of Labor Statistics (BLS,

2023). Since 1994, small businesses have been destined to fail at a rate of

20% within the first 2 years, almost 50% fail within 5 years, and the closure

rates increase at the 10-year mark to 70%. Economic downturns, recessions,

and crises are contributing factors to small business closures (Klundt &

Cooksey, 2023). Safari and Das (2023) determined the root causes of

entrepreneurial failure and noted these attributes included internal and

external factors such as economic policies, internal disputes, education, and

market conditions. However, the most noted reason for small business

failures are due to a source of funding and running out of cash to continue

business operations (Safari & Das, 2023). Being financially literate assists

business owners to manage cash through economic downturns.

The book reviewed in Chapter 2 is broken down into three sections. The first section examined foundational feminist theories that were used as key theories for this research and considered a vital component to the phenomenon of entrepreneurship (Foss et al., 2019). Second was a review of the book to provide readers with a background on entrepreneurship and how the definition has evolved throughout the years to gain a better understanding of what entrepreneurship means in the 21st century. This section also includes a review of book on women entrepreneur types and characteristics, and the gender gaps in entrepreneurship. The final section provides a review of the book on what has been determined as one of the most important skills in entrepreneurship, financial literacy (Burchi et al., 2021). This section delves into what the book says about how financial literacy is defined, what skills are deemed vital to be financially literate, and how financial literacy is measured. The final section also includes an overview of financial technology (fintech) and its benefits and downsides to promoting financial literacy.

Foundational Feminist Theories

Feminist theory reveals the inequities faced by women in the social, economic, political, and legal frames to bring the inequities into consciousness, promote awareness of the inequities, and to find ways to change it (Mohajan, 2022). The theories evolved due to the advocacy of equal rights for women, which are referred to as the waves of feminism. Mohajan (2022) produced a comprehensive paper outlining the four stages of feminism that is discussed later. The term feminism was coined by Charles Fourier, a 19th-century French philosopher as a reaction to the organization of activist groups that supported equality for women (Beecher, 2014). However, his writings took on bizarre twists that were more about love and sexuality and labeled women as sensualities who had gross physical desires (Beecher, 2014). There are many shapes and forms of feminist theory, as indicated by the founder of feminist theory, Mary Wollstonecraft, who authored A *Vindication of the Rights of Women* (1792/2004). Wollstonecraft's book is considered the first liberal feminist work that discussed the suppression of women and is still used in many academic works on feminism (Sangeetha et al., 2022). Feminist theory has gone through many stages to progress equal rights for women. Advocacy of equal rights can be traced back to the inception of the U.S., considered the first wave (1848 through 1920) (Mohajan, 2022), when Abigail Adams, the wife of one of the founding fathers, John Adams, wrote a letter to her husband prior to his signing of the Declaration of Independence to not forget women (Etcheson, 2020). Although her pleas for equality went unaddressed, this lack of rights did not stop women from progressing their own futures. Probably the most familiar victory of the first feminist movement was witnessed at the Seneca Falls Women's Rights Convention in 1848, which was led by Elizabeth Cady Stanton, and eventually led to the passing of the 19th Amendment, which gave the women the right to vote (Allen, 2023). These pioneers of women's advocacy set the stage for women in the upper echelons of society to form closer bonds and exclusive womenonly societies where they would gather and discuss important topics that were limited to them in the public sphere and to attempt to influence change from the top–down.

Almost 40 years later, the second (Mohajan, 2022) wave of feminism took form and ran from the 1960s through the 1970s. The main goals of the second wave of feminism continued the fight for equality but focused on other injustices to women, including rape, reproductive rights, domestic violence, workplace harassment, and education (Hirudayaraj & Shields, 2019). Pivotal to the second wave of feminism was Betty Friedan's (1963) book, *The Feminine Mystique*, which rejected the woman's role as a wife and child bearer. The advocacy of these rights for women led to many laws being passed such as the Equal Pay Act of 1963, which outlawed the gender pay gap; Title IX, (Patsy Mink Equal Opportunity in Education Act, 1972) which gave women the right to educational equality; and the landmark case of *Roe v. Wade* (1973), which gave women the right to reproductive freedom. However, the second wave of feminism did not go on without its critics. Many have said the second wave of feminism was focused on the married woman and did not include equality for women of color (Maxwell & Shields, 2018).

The third wave of feminism (Mohajan, 2022), "championed the inclusion of differences among women and their allies" (Allen, 2023, p. 906). Although the fight for equality was still prevalent, the third wave no longer focused on only white married women. Rather, the movement was intended to embrace diversity in individuals, including differences in race, ethnicity,

sexual orientation, and gender identity (Allen, 2023).

Researchers have studied the topic using three different foundational

feminist theories: (a) feminist empiricism, (b) feminist standpoint theory, and

(c) poststructural feminism. Each of these has its own lens, or different

perspectives, which relate to diverse ways of defining gender equality,

problem constructions, and policy change suggestions (Foss et al., 2019;

Wigginton & Lafrance, 2019). The book for each of these lens in relation to

entrepeneurship is discussed in detail and Table 2.1 highlights the

foundational focus of each.

Table 2.1

*Categories of Feminist Theories Including Feminist Empiricism, Feminist
Standpoint Theory, and Poststructural Feminist Theory*

Theory	View of sex	Notes
Feminist empiricism	Essential (same)	Comparative stance to enforce policies for equality.
Feminist standpoint theory	Essentialist (different)	Women's experiences are unique to them and policies should accommodate the differences.
Poststructuralist feminist theory	Socially constructed	Discrimination is not sex based. It is the result of the social construct and changes over time.

Note. Summary of the views of sex on the three feminist theories discussed in

the research, as indicated by Foss et al. (2019).

Feminist Empiricism

For many years, research on women entrepreneurs has been studied

using feminist empiricism theory, also known as gender-as-a-variable (Foss et al., 2019). Research on entrepreneurship from the feminist empiricist theory takes on a comparative stance between men and women and an essentialist view of sex, in that men and women are the same because they have the same capacities; however, women are not afforded the same opportunities as men. Thus, feminist empiricism is discriminatory in nature (Foss et al., 2019). Cardella et al. (2020) conducted a systematic review of journal articles published on entrepreneurship from 1950 through 2019 and have found the three most common comparative themes in entrepreneurship are (a) financial, political, and social barriers; (b) management practices (characteristics); and (c) performance (profitability, growth).

Critics of feminist empiricism have stated the comparisons that are made have been done so through a male hierarchy; thus, using the male way of thinking and growing a business is viewed from a man's perspective, which does nothing for the empowerment of women entrepreneurs (Foss et al., 2019). In her contribution in a book on feminist studies, Longo (2020) expressed that feminist empiricism examines gender comparisons through power hierarchies, which continue to exacerbate systems of oppression because the methodologies employed are upheld by science. Another criticism of conducting research through feminist empiricism is that there is a lack in descriptive analysis and more use of statistical analysis that has sought to find differences, rather than similarities between men and women entrepreneurs (Henry et al., 2016). Furthermore, feminist empiricism takes the stance that knowledge is based on the experiences through sensory practices, whereby eliminating the social construct and thus relies heavily on replication through scientific rigor and is the process of confirming a hypothesis, theory, or method, which are found in quantitative studies (Allen, 2023; Longo 2020). However, the contributions of research from the feminist empiricism lens have been to promote the gaps in entrepreneurship to enact policies that make entrepreneurship more inclusive to women and promote policy changes (Foss et al., 2019). Empirical research can lead to policy changes. A report authored by Cooper (2021) through the Congressional Research Service used empirical findings to provide the status of financial literacy skills in the U.S. and quoted the use of research to support their findings. Examining entrepreneurship through feminist empiricism has contributed to changes; however, there has been a call for conducting research through qualitative measures (Van Burg et al., 2022).

Feminist Standpoint Theory

The second foundational feminist theory is feminist standpoint theory (FST). FST took shape from the second wave of feminism beginning in the 1960s through the 1970s to becoming a mainstream way of examining women's studies from the perspective or standpoint of the woman (Foss et al., 2019). Foss et al. (2019) conducted a 30-year review on women's entrepreneurship policy research and found that FST was popularized due to the second wave of feminism, which has its roots in social and radical feminism. FST, from any perspective, is the notion that there are individual challenges to cultural values, expectations, and power relationships that lead to subordination or marginalization of a group (Foss et al., 2019). Foss et al. noted that FST views sex from an essentialist view; however, contrary to feminist empiricism, FST views sex as different because women and men are socialized differently. Foss et al. (2019) explained that FST follows the thought that lived experiences of women are unique to them, and men simply cannot understand their lived experiences.

From a policy outcome perspective, FST aims to change the entire social structure to ensure women's needs are included in any outcomes. Some policy implications using FST include quotas being mandated for women-owned businesses, paid paternal leave for parents, not just women, and providing gender-specific training (Foss et al., 2019). FST is viewed from two feminist viewpoints, socialist and radical, with both concentrating on the structure of societal oppression; however, they differ in that socialist feminism questions the structures of capitalism and radical feminism focuses on patriarchal oppression (Foss et al., 2019).

In either form, the goal is to change the entire structure of society to promote inclusiveness and equality. FST has been likened to Hegel's account of the relationship between master and slave in that the relationship can be better understood from the point of view of the slave and a Marxist view of the relationship between the bourgeois and proletariat (Loick, 2023). One of the major critiques of FST is that it focused on common oppressions faced by women in the political sphere, which was predominately from the perspective of the white middle-class woman and omitted the knowledge that can be gained from the perspectives of the differences of women, including class,

race, and socioeconomic status (Harrison et al., 2020). Another critique on

FST is that it sometimes avoids seeking the truth; rather, it is a way for a

group to make their voices heard (Sweet,

2020). Women go through the same struggles and oppression, regardless of

class or race (Harrison et al., 2020). Therefore, just looking at one's social

position negates other factors that may have others think differently. Based

on these critiques, FST eliminates individuality.

Poststructural Feminism

The third foundational feminist theory is poststructural feminist theory

(PSFT). PSFT is an intellectual movement that materialized in the 1980s and

examines how gender is *done*, rather than what it *is* and that gender is

socially constructed, not biological (Ahl & Marlow, 2021). PSFT posits that

acts of discrimination between men and women is not sex-based but a result

of the social construct, which changes over time (Foss et al., 2019; Lather,

1992). Previous research on women entrepreneurship has had a massive

impact on comparative analyses to suggest how women can be *fixed* to adapt

to the male-dominated sphere of entrepreneurship either through training or

policies (Ahl & Nelson, 2015; Foss et al., 2019). Therefore, there is a desire

to investigate women entrepreneurship deficiencies in a different manner,

which is to define women entrepreneurship from the women perspective to

get rid of the presumptions and define women entrepreneurship through their

lived experiences (Ahl & Marlow, 2012). Using the framework of exploring definitions through the lens of the knower can provide different perspectives on what constitutes a deficiency in financial literacy skills of women entrepreneurs versus what is essential for them to know.

PSFT posits there are sources of meanings and interpretation (Maclaran & Stevens, 2019). To highlight this in action it is coherently explained by Andrews (2022), where she used the word *apple* to showcase how words can take on different meanings. Most people would immediately think of fruit; however, if reading an article on actress Gweneth Paltrow, one can see there is a different meaning to the word apple, in that it can also be someone's name. Poststructural theorists remove the structured boundaries that were established by society as a normal way of seeing things. Instead of accepting the status quo, PSFT's main inquiry considers "how we know what we know" (Razack, 1993, p. 95). The main inquiries in PSFT are language and power structures.

One of the main inquiries of poststructuralism is to "scientize language" (Lather, 1992, p. 90). Therefore, for this study, the researcher has determined that asking women entrepreneurs to define financial literacy in their own words follows the major tenet of PSFT. In deconstructing language, one should note the meaning of the word can shift over time and place. The notion is to understand how language is used to create reality, which can then be used to make changes. When Said and Ensline (2020) researched women entrepreneurs, their study prompted responses on the needs and skills required of an entrepreneur, such as empowerment, motivation, business skills, and persistence. In contrast, research by Qazi and Rashidi (2018) wanted to explore the contextual meaning of empowerment from a women's perspective. Both studies captured the lived experiences of entrepreneurs through an open-ended phenomenological approach. However, Qazi and Rashidi (2018) focused on a deeper understanding of the language used.

Overall, feminist theory seeks to address women's societal, political, and legal inequalities. In each stage, a variety of feminist movements have occurred, all with the goal of achieving equality for women. Although there are various lenses of feminist theory, this study focused on PSFT, which aims to understand the inequalities from the perspective of the women entrepreneur.

Entrepreneurship

Throughout history, entrepreneurship has been the backbone of democracy, to reduce poverty, create jobs, and ignite the economy (Lee & Rodriguez-Pos, 2020). There are some notable definitions that can summarize the phenomenon of entrepreneurship. The term entrepreneur was derived from the French meaning *undertaker*, someone who takes something on and gets something done (Thornton, 2020). Economists have been defining entrepreneurship for centuries. Most notable include Richard Cantillon, an IrishFrench economist, who defined entrepreneurship as the process of buying something at present value and then selling the same thing at an uncertain price (Cantillon, 1755/2010). Another economic contributor toward entrepreneurship was Scottish economist Adam Smith. According to research by Graafland and Wells (2021), who examined the work of A. Smith (1789/1981) found that A. Smith's views are focused on one's self-interest and a free market economy, combined with vices and virtues that lead to societal flourishing. Joseph Schumpeter (1934/1949), an Austrian economist, is notably known for his concept of entrepreneurship, which involved the process of *creative destruction*; continuous innovation through new markets, new products, or inventing new ways of manufacturing. Without creative destruction, according to

Schumpeter, stagnation in an economy may lead to its failure. According to Cantillon (1755/1931) and Schumpeter, there are three common components to entrepreneurship that include uncertainty and risk, complemented by managerial competence, creativity, and optimism. Although the definition of entrepreneurship has taken on many iterations, there is a commonality that dates to prestigious economists.

The word entrepreneur and business owner are often seen as interchangeable terms. Researchers have used the terms entrepreneur and business owner interchangeably, blurring the lines of a difference between that of a business owner and entrepreneur (Tripathi et al., 2022). The *newness* definition of entrepreneurship has expanded into what Ratten (2023) called "the identification of business-related opportunities through a process of using existing, new or a recombination of resources in an innovative and creative way" (p. 80). This definition gives new light to an entrepreneurial endeavor in that it not only focuses on business creation as something brand new, but also, it can mean taking an existing business to new levels. Although these definitions have come from economists since the early 15th century, the one thing in common is the ability to create economic growth through a democracy.

Aside from the economists' perspective, others have defined entrepreneurship in various ways. According to the U.S. Chamber of Commerce (2022), an entrepreneur can be a solopreneur, one who owns and operates a business as a sole employee. Others refer to entrepreneurs as gig workers or freelancers; those who are employed by others but have a side business (Marx et al., 2023). A working paper authored by Christnacht et al. (2018) from the U.S. Census Bureau defined an entrepreneur as someone who is selfemployed and a business owner. The U.S. Census Bureau (2023) has relabeled its reporting from the Annual Survey of Entrepreneurs to the Annual Business Survey and even added solopreneurs to its reporting structure.

The BLS (2018) refers to an entrepreneur as a person who owns a business and produces annual information through the annual business employment dynamics set of statistics. Jeff Bezos' entrepreneurial endeavor can be viewed as following the Schumpeter (1934/1949) school of thought because he revolutionized ecommerce by creating an innovative marketplace (Dutta, 2018) and fell under the descriptive term of a unicorn. Unicorns are entrepreneurs that have companies that are privately held businesses that are valued over $1 billion or more and seek funding through venture capitalists or private investors (Chen, 2024). For example, the high-growth and highly valued privately held businesses unicorns start out by using scalable business models using technology, devote investments in research and development, and typically use investors (Cristofaro et al., 2024), similar to Jeff Bezos. This is an example of how an entrepreneur can be a solo-operated business and grow into multibillion dollar enterprises. Business owners who operate a business in an existing industry may not fall under the *newness* category. However, one thing remains the same, to be an entrepreneur, regardless of size, takes risk (Tripathi et al., 2022). This supports that there is no longer a delineation between the two terms entrepreneur and business owner.

In addition to BLS and the U.S. Census Bureau, there are other sources of entrepreneurship data. The Global Entrepreneurship Monitor (GEM; Hill et al., 2023), started in 1999 as a joint research project between Babson College and London Business School, have been publishing information on entrepreneurship characteristics, motivations, and demographics annually for over 23 years. GEM defined entrepreneurship as a means of improving lives through the creation of jobs through the efforts of an ideation process of creating new goods and services. The latest GEM report (Hill et al., 2023) specified entrepreneurial activity in three ways: (a) the nascent entrepreneur, (b) new business owner, and (c) established business owner. This data source also uses the two terms "entrepreneur" and "business owner" interchangeably.

Reporting and labeling an entrepreneur have changed shape. Business owners, solopreneurs, gig workers, freelancers, and those who own an established business now fall under the umbrella of an entrepreneur. The data indicated the Schumpeterian (1934/1949) school of thought is still prevalent, but the definition of entrepreneurship has changed. With the use of so many differing definitions of entrepreneurs, there is one thing in common; all the reporting agencies typically refer to these different forms of entrepreneurship as small businesses.

Small Businesses

Throughout the 20th century, the U.S. government undertook many initiatives to enhance entrepreneurship and assist with funding small ventures. To recognize the economic value that small businesses brought to the U.S., the government enacted the Small Business Act in 1953, which intended to promote free enterprise competition through government contracts, financial, technical, and management support to small businesses and in the same year, the Small Business Administration (SBA, n.d.b) was formed to uphold the laws outlined in the Small Business Act (Office of the Comptroller of the Currency, n.d.). Since then, there have been varying definitions of a small business. The BLS (2018) defined an establishment with less than 100 employees as a small business. The SBA defined a small business based on three criteria: (a) industry, (b) sales receipts, and (c) number of employees. Industry and sales receipts vary; however, the number of employees is typically met by 500 or less. This includes businesses that operate with one or no employees (SBA, 2023j). The Organization of

Economic Cooperation and Development (OECD, 2023) defines a small

business as an enterprise with less than 250 employees. The OECD has

continued to subdivide businesses and labels enterprises with less than 10

employees as a microenterprise. Research also deciphers small business in

terms of micro and macro businesses whereby "micro" describes an

individual business function and "macro" is about clusters or industry

(Gianiodis et al., 2022). Many agencies have delineated the meaning of a

small business, which is mostly done for different funding opportunities

(SBA, n.d.b).

Microenterprise

The term microenterprise was developed by Yunus (2007), who sought

for a way to help local small businesses gain access to capital to increase

entrepreneurship in Bangladesh. In 2007, the U.S. amended the Small

Business Act to include provisions for microenterprises, which are

recognized as businesses with less than 5 employees and introduced the

Microloan Amendments and Modernization Act. The program was enacted to

specifically assist disenfranchised entrepreneurs with access to capital to start

a business. Among the disenfranchised are women, veterans, and minorities

(Microloan Amendments and Modernization Act, 2007). Microenterprises, on

average, earn less than $50,000 annually, and require a small amount of

capital to start and grow their business, and they are typically solo-owned

businesses or freelancers. They make up 92% of businesses in the U.S, and they are the most vulnerable to financial instability, especially during

exogenous shocks, including the COVID-19 pandemic (S. Liu & Parilla,

2020; Miklian & Hoelscher, 2022; Prosperity Now, 2020). There are over 12

million women entrepreneurs in the U.S., with 10.8 million having no

employees and are informally known as solopreneurs, a venture that is owned

and operated by the owner (Varma,

2023).

As microenterprises make up most businesses, loan disbursements to

microenterprises are far less than small businesses; billions of dollars to small

businesses versus $300 million to microenterprises (McCay, 2014). The

average microloan, according to the SBA (2023d), is $13,000. A contributing

factor, as noted by a report published by the Consultation Group to Assist the

Poor, indicated the use of financial jargon is a reason microenterprises cannot

gain access to finance (Sawhney, 2022). According to a survey by the Center

for Financial and Economic Decision Making, now known as Prosperity

Now, microenterprises indicated they only had enough funds to sustain their

business for 1 month (McKay, 2014). There also has been research that

indicated the development of the categorization of microenterprises is

detrimental because it further divides microenterprises as underfunded,

mostly made up of women, and further sets them apart from the mainstream

business world (Ehlers & Main, 1998).

There is also a gender gap in the earnings of microentrepreneurs as

reported by the Association of Entrepreneur Opportunities (AEO, 2013). The

AEO reported on the statistics of microenterprises, which are businesses that have less than 5 employees, and indicated 92% of small businesses fall under the definition of a microenterprise, and are categorized into five categories: (a) newcomers; (b) part-time, not primary income; (c) part-time, primary income; (d) full-time, less than $50,000 in sales; and (e) full-time, $50,000 or more in sales, and the gap increases as more money is made. The participants in this study fall under all the categories except for Category 1, newcomers, because the participants have been in business for 5 or more years. Table 2.2 is a depiction of the gender gap in earnings across the four categories of microenterprises as reported by AEO

(2013).

Table 2.2

Gender Disparity in Earnings of Microenterprises

Category	Male	Female
Type 2: Part-time, not primary income	48%	30%
Type 3: Part-time, primary income	44%	37%
Type 4: Full-time, less than $50k in sales	49%	32%
Type 5: Full-time more than $50k in sales	61%	18%

Note. These data were obtained from the AEO (2013). In 2024, AEO updated the data and changed their reporting standards on microenterprises and define a microenterprise as a small business with 0 to 9 employees. By making this change, the AEO reported the number of microenterprises is 96%, which is not comparable to the 2013 report. Furthermore, the AEO has not reported on the earnings gender gap at the new definition of a microenterprise.

In addition to the earnings gap reported by the AEO in 2013, a survey conducted by FreshBooks, in conjunction with Research NOW (2018), supported the findings of a gap in earnings in entrepreneurship. According to the report, the self-employment wage gap stands at 28% with men earning, on average $77,540 versus $56,184 for women (FreshBooks, 2018). Some noteworthy results of the Women in the Independent Workforce Report by FreshBooks (2018) indicated 20% of women stated they must charge less than their male counterparts to acquire or retain clients, 30% indicated they are not taken seriously, and an additional 30% indicated they must work harder than men that do the same job. Because microenterprises make up most small businesses, gender gaps should be better understood so that policies can continue to provide support to them.

Women Entrepreneurs

Until 1976, with the publication of the first journal article by Schwartz, there was no differentation in the phenomenon of entrepreneurship based on gender (Yadav & Unni, 2016). Two years later, in 1979, the SBA developed a separate section for women business owners known as the Office of Women's Business Ownership, which provided resources for the underserved demographic such as business training, counseling, and access to credit and federal contracts (SBA, 2023i). In 1979, the U.S. government also published its first report on women entrepreneurship entitled *The Bottom Line: Unequal*

Enterprise in America. (U.S. Department of Congress, 1978). This was the first report published by the U.S. government acknowledging the gaps of entrepreneurship, which was advocated for by the National Association of Women Business Owners (NAWBO), established in 1975 (NAWBO, n.d.a). The U.S Department of Congress (1978) reported there were gaps in "financing, education, management training and technical assistance and in sex stereotyping and discrimination" (p. 6). The goals of the Small Business Act were to bridge the gap between genders, which intended to legally ban discrimination in lending to women business owners (NAWBO, n.d.b). Although it seemed gender inequalities in entrepreneurship were being addressed, there was still much to do.

In 1988, the SBA established the Women's Business Center Program, which provided state level assistance to women business owners who continued to face discriminatory barriers (SBA, 2023f). Although women entrepreneurs have been in existence for quite some time in U.S. history, it was not until 1988 when women were able to secure funding for their ventures without a man's signature nationally (Wolfe, 2018). In 1988, Ronald Reagan signed into law the Women's Business Ownership Act, which eliminated any state laws that required a male relative to cosign for a business loan. Before that point, several states continued to require a man to cosign on any business loans for a women-led businesses. However, Harrison et al. (2020) stated, "Entrepreneurship policies targeted at women are contributing little or nothing to their equality, well-being, or independence" (p. 1045).

Henry et al. (2022) agreed with the research by Harrison et al. (2020) and

highlighted that although there is an abundance of policies on women's

entrepreneurship in general terms, which focus on deficiencies of women, or

report on the state of affairs in women entrepreneurship, "few have focused

on policies to increase women entrepreneurs'access to financial capital"

(Henry et al., 2022,

p. 230). Henry et al. argued that more emphasis is needed on policies that

promote access to financial capital rather than focusing on the shortfalls of

women entrepreneurs based on men's performance.

Characteristics of Women Entrepreneurs

Historically, entrepreneurs have been associated with masculine

attributes such as risk taking. Entrepreneurship follows in the same man-

dominated realm whereby commercial and social entrepreneurship have been

positively correlated with perceptions of masculinity (Bullough et al., 2022;

Gupta et al., 2022). These perceptions are generally guided by societal norms.

There has been scant evidence of the characteristics of entrepreneurs in

the past decade (2012 through 2022) in the U.S. (Yangailo & Qutieshat,

2022). According to a systematic book review by Yangailo and Qutieshat

(2022), there have been seven studies on the topic of dominant entrepreneurial

characteristics, all being conducted quantitatively. Four focused on

entrepreneurial success and the remaining three were on entrepreneurial

intentions (Yangailo & Qutieshat, 2022). Of the seven studies, the top

characteristics included (a) self-efficacy, (b)

consciousness, (c) locus of control, (d) need for achievement, and (e) innovativeness. Conscientiousness was further reiterated as a characteristic through the findings of a survey of 204 small-to-medium sized businesses, which indicated that paying attention to the business resulted in positive performances such as increased revenues, profits, sales, customers, and product lines (Waziri & Nnko, 2023). According to Kuratko et al. (2021), the characteristics of an entrepreneur are defined as having a distinct mindset. Kuratko et al. (2021) defined the entrepreneurial mindset into three aspects: (a) the cognitive mindset, which examines the mental acuity of an entrepreneur; (b) behavioral characteristics, which examines how the behaviors of an entrepreneur drive opportunities; and (c) emotions, which examines how one feels about being an entrepreneur. These mindsets are expanded upon in the next section.

The cognitive mindset in entrepreneurship is the mental ability to take unconnected information and piece it together to make decisions (Kuratko et al., 2021) and the cognitive mindset makes no differentiation between men and women entrepreneurs. However, according to research by Shmailan (2016), decision making was found to be a characteristic that does differ between men and women, in that men make quicker decisions. The differences in characteristics between men and women entrepreneurs is discussed further from findings by Shmailan (2016).

Expanding on behavioral characteristics, Maczolskij and Vijnikaien (2023) found that confidence is strongly related to more profitable ventures.

A report published by the 2020 GEM (Elam et al., 2021) indicated that there is a research gap in self-efficacy among men and women entrepreneurs, and Jennings et al. (2023) has indicated the findings of the gender gap are based on the reference to men entrepreneurs as being the standard measure of confidence. Although the study by Jennings et al. (2023) indicated that women scored lower in self-efficacy, this finding is not suggestive of women entrepreneurs being underconfident or resulting in women having a deficiency. Rather, having an overabundance of confidence was found to have a detrimental impact on ventures that were unfamiliar to the entrepreneurs (2023).

Further elaborating on Kuratko et al.'s (2021) entrepreneurial mindsets, emotions play a role. As an example, the emotion of passion is not a financial skill; however, it has been correlated to entrepreneurial performance and considered essential to entrepreneurship (Cardon et al., 2009) and has been supported by Hu et al. (2022). Hu et al. (2022) studied entrepreneurial passion from the woman's perspective and concluded that women entrepreneurs who pay attention to their passion can lead to successful ventures. Additionally, higher levels of passion are positively and strongly related to entrepreneurial intentions (Kyriakopoulos et al., 2024). However, others claim the characteristics and traits are more self-centered, claiming an entrepreneur has "more energy than the normal person and are hard workers" (Shmailan, 2016, p. 2). The problem with this definition is that it can be applied to anyone, under any circumstance. Shmailan's (2016) research is broken down into five main traits associated with entrepreneurship that coincide with the previous descriptions and include: (a) decisionmaking styles, (b) risk tolerance, (c) financing decisions for the business, (d) management styles, and (e) networking. Table 2.3 is a high-level summary of the five differences in characteristics of men and women entrepreneurs according to Shmailan.

Table 2.3

General Characteristics of Men and Women Entrepreneurs

Characteristic	Men	Women
Decision making	Easier	More difficult
Risk tolerance	Propensity for risk	Risk averse
Financing	More capital, more debt	Less capital, less debt
Management styles	Logical thinkers, more aggressive about expansion	Intuitive thinkers, cautious and conservative about expansion
Networking	Larger networks	Smaller networks

Note. The data included in this table are a summary of Shmailan's (2016) findings.

The following section delves deeper into what book says about the five characteristics identified by Shmailan (2016).

Decision-Making Ability

Decision making is a critical skill that is part of every day life (Morelli et al., 2022) and even more so in a business environment. McKinsey and Company (2023) reported that executives spend at least 40% of their time making decisions. Entrepreneurs are faced with several aspects of decision making, including taking advantage of opportunities, exploiting opportunities, and even making decisions about entry and exit strategies in entrepreneurship (Morelli et al., 2022). According to Shmailan (2016), men entrepreneurs have the ability to make decisions quicker than women and they require less information when making decisions because their focus is on keeping costs under control to raise profits. On the other side, Shmailan described women entrepreneurs as democratic thinkers whereby it takes them longer to make decisions because they are not only concerned with positive outcomes for their business, they are also concerned about the growth of others.

Carranza et al. (2018) backed up Shmailan's claim that it takes women longer to make decisions because they typically, more so than men, have to intertwine their personal and professional lives. Therefore, the woman entrepreneur does not only worry about business decisions, but she also has to worry about family decisions. Research has also indicated that outsourcing functions of the business for decision making can have positive impacts on the business (Fomina & Kolomiiets, 2022). Fomina and Kolomiiets (2022) have found that outsourcing certain functions of the business, such as accounting and bookkeeping, can have positive impacts including minimizing costs, increasing the correctness and accuracy of numbers to protect businesses from fines, provide for tax optimization, and provides professional advice for the business owners, which can take the burden off of the business owner in making decisions on areas where they may not be as proficient.

Shmailan's (2016) research did not place decision making under any context except for the intention of starting a business. Decision making in enterpreneurship spans this one topic. According to Shepherd et al. (2015), decision making can differ when conditions are uncertain and certain, meaning that decision making could change depending on the entrepreneur's knowledge of the decision that has to be made (i.e., if the decision that has to be made is about an entrepreneur's customer, decisions can be made differently based on the entrepreneur's knowledge of their consumer). Additionally, Shepherd et al. (2015) added the entrepreneur's emotions can be a contributing factor to the speed of decision making and market conditions. Rather than a comparative stance on women and men entrepreneurs, Shepherd et al. (2015) found that unfavorable market conditions could diminish decision-making options. Although decision making may be different between men and women entrepreneurs for starting a business, there is evidence that concludes there are conditions where decision making in entrepreneurship is dependent upon other factors.

Risk Tolerance

The foundation of determining a person's willingness to monopolize off of uncertainty can be traced back to 1954. Daniel Bernoulli (1954) published a paper on risk taking using the well-known coin toss outcomes, whereby wagers were set on whether a flipped coin would end up on heads or tails. If the outcome was favorable with the participant's prediction, they would double their initial wager (Bernoulli, 1954). The opposite of risk tolerance is risk aversion, which is avoiding uncertainty. According to

Shmailan (2016), men entrepreneurs are risk tolerant and women

entrepreneurs are less risk tolerant. However, Koudstaal et al. (2016) found

that entrepreneurs, in general, are less risk averse than a waged employee.

Therefore, regardless of gender, entrepreneurs seek to minimize their risks.

According to other researchers, women entrepreneurs were found to be

more risk averse than men (Artz, 2017; Carranza et al., 2018). In a qualitative

study by Kappal and Rastogi (2020), they indicated that women

entrepreneurs were more willing to take risks with the business but were less

risk averse when it came to investing because the participants stated they

were not well-versed in understanding investing. However, if they did, they

stated they would be more prone to take more risks on long-term investments.

Manolova et al. (2020) challenged the notion of women entrepreneurs being

more afraid of taking on risks than men. Manolova et al. based this on how

quickly women entrepreneurs were able to pivot their business models when

the COVID-19 pandemic impacted the world. Manolova et al.'s research

indicated that women were able to offer new products and services and

change their business strategies including having a virtual office or offering

online classes. Manolova et al. indicated that women entrepreneurs were able

to pivot their business model to reduce risk and realize new business

opportunities. Other researchers have indicated there is not enough evidence

to support the myth of women being more risk averse due to the flawed way

in which risk aversion is measured in entrepreneurship (Hambock et al.,

2017; Morgenroth et al., 2020). Measuring ris aversion is similar to the way financial literacy is assessed, which is through self-assessments and quantitative measurements.

Financing

Various research has shown there is a gender gap in access to financing in entrepreneurship (Pitchbook, 2024; U.S. Senate Committee on Small Business & Entrepreneurship, 2023). Women entrepreneurs are 63% less likely than men in acquiring external funding (Guzman & Kacperczyk, 2019). According to Shmailan (2016), when it comes to financing, men and women entrepreneurs are on the opposite ends of the spectrum. Shmailan purports that men-led businesses have more capital and more debt, and women-led businesses have less capital and less debt. Other researchers (Cardella et al., 2020; Robichaud et al., 2019) have concluded the same findings in that women entrepreneurs begin their businesses with less capital and secure financing through informal or familial channels.

When acquiring a loan, women entrepreneurs receive less funding than men. This is supported by the nonprofit organization SCORE (2019), a resource partner with the SBA, who indicated that women-owned small businesses rely on personal savings, a second job, or family and friends to fund their business operations. However, funding operations without taking on loans has revealed that there is an advantage to women's empowerment. Daher et al. (2022) found the impacts of savings on microenterprises revealed an advantage to savings over microcredit programs, which has facilitated women's empowerment and has a significant impact on their psychosocial well-being. The study added that having savings heightens financial inclusion without having to go into debt (Daher et al., 2022). Therefore it can be viewed as a positive benefit to rely on family or friends and savings, rather than going through formal channels offered to microenterprises. Robichaud et al. (2019) have found that women microentrepreneurs in the service, retail, and food services sectors were scrutinized more so than entrepreneurs in general.

Women entrepreneurs who received funding from an all-women venture capitalist are less likely to receive a second round of funding if they pitched for a second round from male venture capitalists (Solal & Snellman, 2023). Solal and Snellman (2023) conducted an experiment using master in business administraton students who pitched a fictional startup idea for a second round of funding. The results indicated that if the women entrepreneurs stated initial funding came from a woman, they were less likely to be approved for a second round of funding, regardless of the gender of the venture capitalist. Solal and Snellman credited this to attribution bias whereby venture capitalists who found out the initial funding came from a man, the instinct of the investor was that the women founder was more competent and the business was stronger. This is another example of the gender gaps in financing and could be a contributing factor of why women entrepreneurs tend to seek financing from family and friends.

Contrary to research that indicated there is a gender gap in financing (Pitchbook, 2024; U.S. Senate Committee on Small Business & Entrepreneurship, 2023), Kwapisz and Hechavarria (2018) found there is not necessarily a gap in financing becuase women entrepreneurs sometimes intentionally do not ask for external financing due to the type of business, which are typically smaller and are in less profitable industries. Research by Hewa-Wellalage et al. (2021) found there was indeed a gender bias in credit during the COVID-19 pandemic. Women entrepreneurs received more assistance with cash flow problems. Hewa-Wellalage et al. (2021) also found there was no gender bias in equity financing during the same period.

Despite the contrary research results of there being no gender gaps in access to financing for entrepreneurs (Kwapisz & Hechavarria, 2018), the evidence is scant and the proof of the gender gaps can be found in the numbers regarding lending. Women entrepreneurs received only 2% from venture capitalists in 2020, a decrease from 2019 (D. Davis, 2023). Men entrepreneurial businesses are approved for loans more often, receive more external funding, and are less impacted during a crisis (Pitchbook, 2024; U.S. Senate Committee on Small Business & Entrepreneurship, 2023). Table 2.4 provides some statistical evidence to back up these claims.

Table 2.4

Lending Information on Small Businesses

Category		Source
Men	Women	

Loan Denials[a]	19%	25%	U.S. Senate Committee on Small Business Entrepreneurship (2023)
SBA 7(a) Loan Approvals[b]	67.4%	21.2%	U.S. SBA (2023g)
SBA 504 Loan Approvals[c]	63.1%	14.9%	U.S. SBA (2023e)

Note. [a]Loan denial percentages data from 2022.

[b]SBA 7(a) loans are for smaller businesses and loans cannot exceed $5 million and are intended to be used to for smaller projects including refinancing current debt or furniture purchases (SBA, 2023g).

[c]SBA loan data as of December 14, 2023. SBA 504 loans are fixed rate loans that cannot exceed $5.5 million and must be used for major fixed assets (SBA, 2023e.).

In summary, to start a business requires some sort of financial resources and it is considered one of the most critical financial decisions an entrepreneur can face (SBA, 2023c). Therefore, even if the women entrepreneur goes through different channels to secure financing for their business, knowing what is available can help to close the gender gap found in financing.

Management Styles

According to Shmailan (2016), entrepreneurs have differed in their management styles in how they think and how they view growth ambitions. Shmailan posited that women entrepreneurs have a feminist way of thinking, which is the notion of putting the thoughts of their employees above everything else. Shmailan stated that women are more intuitive in their thinking styles versus men, who are more logical in their thinking styles. Before delving into the different management styles of entrepreneurs, this section takes a closer look at logical and intuitive thinking. According to Wimmer et al. (2022), intuitive thinking is associated with strategic thinking and balancing goals. It is the cognitive process of using *one's gut instinct* to make decisions, which typically leads to quicker decisions (Koudstaal et al., 2019). This is contrary to the decision-making skills indicated by Shmailan (2016). Koudstaal et al. (2019) also indicated that entrepreneurs, in general, think more intuitively than managers.

On the other side are logical thinkers. Logical thinkers are those who assemble the facts before making a decision and avoid using their emotions (Doyle, 2021). Overall, the major differences between intuitive and logical differences are that one leads to rapid judgments and decision making (intuitive), and the other leads to slower and deliberate decision making (logical). According to Shmailan (2016), the decision-making abilities of entrepreneurs are quite contrary to Doyle's definition of logical and intuitive thinking. One can argue that decision-making abilities are a different category of management styles altogether. According to Miranda (2023), management styles involve how one works with a team, plans projects, sets and measures goals, and delegates work. Some characteristics include communication skills, values about relationships, and leadership traits

(Miranda, 2023). These management styles can lean into a leadership form (Raza & Siddiqui, 2023), and there are various leadership styles.

The most prevalent leadership style of women entrepreneurs is the transformative style (Raza & Siddiqui, 2023). The transformative leadership style is the ability to inspire and empower employees, which leads to an increase in morale and a healthier work environment, leading to a more productive business. According to Shmailan's (2016) comparative review of traits and characteristics of men and women entrepreneurs, he stated that men entrepreneurs are more task oriented, which is in line with a transactional leadership style (Afsar et al., 2017). Transactional leadership is similar to an authoritarian style of leadership in that the entrepreneur sets out goals, tasks, expectations and uses a reward and punishment system as a key motivator (Afsar et al., 2017). Research has indicated that men entrepreneurs use the transactional style of leadership more often than women entrepreneurs (Hassan & Hashim, 2015). Although the management styles of men and women may differ, research has shown that each have the same goal of establishing, running, and growing a business. Entrepreneurs, in general, find ways to monopolize opportunities and communicate the validity, strength, and value of their business (Laguia et al., 2019).

Networking

Networking has been found to be an important characteristic in entrepreneurship, as it can help to build relationships to acquire resources in the form of funding, skills, and business services (Redd & Wu, 2020).

Shmailan (2016) claimed networking abilities are different between men and women entrepreneurs, with men having larger networks than women, which could be a contributor to the poor performance of women entrepreneurs. Shmailan described the meaning of *larger* as being more robust and penetrative into business networks. Although this may be true, Redd and Wu (2020) examined the differences of networking using online social networking platforms and differentiated networking connections by weak or familial, with weaker connections (not family or friends) being more beneficial for an entrepreneur. The results of Redd and Wu's (2020) study have concluded that women entrepreneurs have statistically significantly more weak ties than men. Additionally, K. Smith et al. (2018) also substantiated Redd and Wu's results and found that as a women entrepreneur's business progresses, she begins to broaden her networks by forming weaker ties. Although women entrepreneurs may start their businesses with smaller networks that consist of family and friends, as indicated by Shmailan (2016), other research has indicated that women's networking broadens as the business progresses. The importance of networking is also emphasized by (I. Liu, 2023) as reported by The Milken Institute's 27th Annual Global Conference, indicating that networks are vital to women entrepreneurs as they can provide mentorship and guidance to a company founder.

In addition to networking with others, research has indicated that collaborating with competition is another form of networking (Johnson &

Mehta, 2024). Qualitative research conducted by Johnson and Mehta (2024) found cooperating with others resulted in monetary and nonmonetary benefits. As an example, a nonmonetary benefit included social benefits, which resulted in confidence in the participants. Also, it led to a broader network of resources, which can all lead to monetary benefits.

Women Entrepreneur Industries

Although women entrepreneurship is on the rise, gender continues to play a role in the industries that are dominated by women entrepreneurs because the phenomenon of entrepreneurship is still defined by gender role expectations (Bullough et al., 2022). The sectors that are dominated by women microentrepreneurs include data from GEM (Hill et al., 2023), which showed that the top three industries occupied by women entrepreneurs are the wholesale or retail sector, business and consumer goods, and government and social services. These sectors are characterized by lower entry barriers, have a heavy reliance on consumers as customers (rather than other businesses) and are extremely competitive, which makes them among the most vulnerable in most economies, especially during a crisis (World Economic Forum, 2020). Additionally, the U.S. Census Bureau (2022) listed the top three industries owned by women as healthcare and social services; professional, scientific, and technical services; and retail trade. One of the contributing factors to these specific industries is due to the familial obligations that are placed upon women through culture and society, with women having to take on more responsibilities than men (Bullough et al.,

2022). As indicated by Bullough et al., it has always been the *norm* that

women tended to the home, and men worked outside of the home, thus,

limiting their opportunities to have a business as an income generator.

Another contributor as to why women entrepreneurs gravitate toward smaller

and less profitable business is the link to their educational backgrounds,

whereby women typically enter the fields of education, sociology, language,

and the social sciences (Office on the Economic Status of Women, 2016).

Table 2.5 represents a statistical breakdown of bachelor degrees that were

awarded by sex in the 2020 through 2021 academic year as reported by the

National Center for Education Statistics (Irwin et al., 2023).

Table 2.5

*Percentage Distribution of Bachelor's Degrees Conferred by Degree-
Granting Postsecondary Institutions in Selected Fields of Study, by Sex:
Academic Year 2020 through 2021*

Selected field of study	Men	Women
Health profession and related programs	15%	85%
Psychology	20%	80%
Biological and biomedical services	34%	66%
Social sciences and history	48%	52%
Business	53%	47%
Engineering	76%	24%

Note. Data were from a report by Irwin et al. (2023) published for the U.S. Department of

Education) and disseminated through the National Center for Education Statistics.

The choices made by women entrepreneurs to enter into low-income and lowgrowth occupations are sometimes made by choice and research has indicated that this should, by no means, be attributed to women entrepreneurs underperforming or deem them as being unsuccessful (Office on the Economic Status of Women, 2016).

COVID-19 Pandemic Impact on Women Entrepreneurs

Previous sections in the book review have indicated the gender inequalities that women entrepreneurs face in the U.S. In concert with the identified gender gaps in entrepreneurship, the COVID-19 pandemic brought about new challenges for all of humanity, including economic, social, environmental, educational, and health setbacks (Miyah et al., 2022). As this research focused on gender gaps in entrepreneurship, this section focuses on the economic impacts to women entrepreneurs during this time. Much of the book that discusses the impacts of economic downturns and natural disasters (i.e., crises) have found that smaller and less capitalized firms were the most impacted (Bartik et al., 2020; Srjoh et al., 2022).

The COVID-19 pandemic impacted the world, and research has shown that women entrepreneurs were impacted more than men for various reasons (Manolova et al., 2020). Manolova et al. (2020) concluded that because women entrepreneurs' businesses are younger, smaller, and occupy industries that were severely impacted by the pandemic, they were disproportionately impacted by the crisis. Manolova et al. went on to say that women were more impacted than men due to how each responded to and prepared for crises, whereby woman take a defensive approach and men take on an offensive approach. Manolova et al. articulated how women entrepreneurs faced significant work and family balance issues, as schools were mandated to shut down and women had to take on the responsibilities of running the household (Brieger et al., 2023; Power, 2020). Women-owned businesses were also impacted by loss of income, and they had more business closures than men; 30% of closures for women-owned businesses versus 17% of men-owned business (Goldstein et al., 2022; Manolova et al., 2020).

Industries mostly occupied by women entrepreneurs make them more vulnerable to business failure, which was the case during COVID-19. More specific, the sectors that were most impacted negatively by the pandemic included restaurants and bars, travel, retail, and personal services, which are predominately owned and operated by women entrepreneurs (Choi et al., 2022). Aside from business failures due to industries mostly occupied by women entrepreneurs, they were also adversely affected due to the life and work balance conflict, whereby women had to take on more family responsibilities thus, leading them to devote less time to run their business (Goldstein et al., 2022). Goldstein et al. (2022) focused on the impact of the pandemic in regard to increased childcare responsibilities on women entrepreneurs. Due to school closures and increased family obligations, the pandemic forced many women to either devote less time to their ventures or close them down permantly.

There has been other evidence of growth in gender inequalities among women entrepreneurs due to the COVID-19 pandemic (Fisher & Ryan, 2021), which has impacted women entrepreneurs disproportionally and has been coined as the *she-cession* (Holpuch, 2021). One reason for the she-cession cited in the book was the pandemic's impact on nonessential businesses, which are predominately owned and operated by women entrepreneurs (Han, 2021). To assist small businesses during the pandemic, Congress passed a relief bill for small business owners (SBOs) titled the Paycheck Protection Program (PPP) loan (U.S. Department of the Treasury, n.d.). The purpose of the PPP loan program was to assist SBOs with monetary resources for job retention and other expenses to help businesses survive during the pandemic, which would be forgiven if eligibility requirements were met (U.S. Department of the Treasury,

n.d.). According to the SBA (2021a), approximately 1.1 million PPP loans were approved for women-owned businesses versus 1.7 million loans approved for men-owned businesses. The distributed dollar amount equated to approximately $33 billion versus $90 billion, respectively (SBA, 2021a). Furthermore, SBOs that requested a PPP loan between $150,000 and $350,000 were dispersed to 82% of men-owned businesses, compared to 18% of women-owned businesses (Kickul et al., 2021). The loan approval amount and financial disbursements were in line with the gender gap that women entrepreneurs have faced with receiving external funding.

Financial Literacy

Whether one is a consumer or business owner, financial literacy has been documented as being an important asset for every individual's well-being (Burchi et al., 2021; Lusardi, 2015). The following section discusses the various definitions of financial literacy and its importance to individuals, businesses, the economy, and society. The section also includes how financial literacy is measured, which has contributed toward the gender gap in entrepreneurship. Also included is an analysis, based on the book, to determine whether the introduction of fintech tools is helping or hindering financial literacy.

Financial Literacy Definitions

Financial literacy is defined in many ways by policy makers, government institutions, organizations, and scholars. The OECD (2023) defined financial literacy as having awareness, knowledge, skills, and behaviors to make financial decisions to achieve individual well-being. Similarly, a research report by the U.S. Congress in 2021 added knowledge of the "tools that equip people to make individual financial decisions and take action to attain their goals" (Cooper, 2021, p. 3) as another layer of financial literacy. The Corporate Finance Institute (n.d.) defined financial literacy in more specific terms such as knowing about budgeting, taxation, investing, and borrowing. Lusardi (2015), one of the creators of financial literacy assessments that are used globally, defined financial literacy as an, "ability to process economic information and make informed decisions about financial planning, wealth accumulation, debt, and pensions" (p. 260). Although there are many definitions and uses of financial literacy, the common themes in these definitions are knowledge, behaviors, abilities, and action.

The Importance of Financial Literacy

The importance of financial literacy spans from an individual's financial wellbeing and readiness for retirement (Lusardi, 2015) to an essential skillset for an entrepreneur. Financial literacy is considered one of the most important attributes that contribute to entrepreneurial success (Burchi et al., 2021; Nitani et al., 2020) and to a nation's economic stability (Lusardi & Mitchell, 2014). Worldwide, the importance of financial literacy has led the OECD (2022) to develop a toolkit that has been approved and used by G20 countries since 2013 to assess a country's financial literacy, inclusion, resilience, and well-being. The toolkit is a quantitative measurement and includes categories of risk diversification, inflation, numeracy, and compound interest (OECD, 2022). The categories that are included in the OECD toolkit come from existing surveys, specifically, the *Big Five* questionnaire test developed by Mitchell and Lusardi (2022), which was first used to measure one's readiness for retirement.

Although there have been initiatives to increase financial literacy in the U.S. by the government, dating back to the 1950s and 1960s (Hastings et al., 2013), it was not until 2022 when the National Conference of State Legislatures passed legislation in 37 states, Guam, Puerto Rico, and the District of Columbia, mandating financial literacy into primary school curriculums (Morton, 2022; National Conference of State Legislatures,

2022). Although financial literacy is of importance, Fernandes et al. (2014)

found that those who had undertaken a financial literacy course in school had

forgotten the information learned within 20 months; therefore, financial

literacy teachings should be taught with a *just-in-time* mentality, meaning, it

should be taught when it is needed (Fernandes et al., 2014). Fernandes et al.

suggested that financial literacy in schools should err on soft skills such as

the propensity for planning. Furthermore, it has been found that educators in

general are not prepared to teach financial topics (Henning & Lucey, 2017;

Jayaraman et al., 2022). Henning and Lucey (2017) found that educators had

no experience at all in teaching financial literacy, and Jayaraman et al. (2022)

revealed that 81% of teachers ranked themselves through a self-assessment of

financial literacy skills as moderate to low.

There are several authors who disputed the findings by Fernandes et al.

(2014), including Kaiser and Menkhoff (2020) who have conducted a study

on financial education on students in school and revealed a positive effect on

improved financial literacy test scores. Furthermore, the adoption of

interactive-based teachings of financial literacy in the classroom has shown to

have statistically significant improvements in students' financial literacy

(Batty et al., 2020; Totenhagen et al., 2015). My Classroom Economy is a

simulated-based program that is used throughout the school day, providing

students with real-time rewards and fines throughout the day, including

paying rent for a desk and earning a salary for completing tasks (Batty et al.,

2020; Totenhagen et al., 2015). Overall, the book revealed that financial literacy should be taught. However, there are still debates on how to go about properly instituting programs that are effective (Totenhagen et al., 2015). Totenhagan et al.'s results were based on a pilot study and have shown a statistically significant improvement in students' financial knowledge. Renowned author on financial literacy, Lusardi (2019) vehemently disagreed with Fernandes et al.'s claims and reiterated the importance of financial literacy in education in that the exposure to young people prepares them for financial decision making and it provides access to financial literacy to those that may never be exposed to it (e.g., underserved populations, women). Lusardi (2019) did not call for financial literacy education at the high school level only. Rather, Lusardi called for financial literacy education throughout one's life (e.g., primary education, college, the workplace).

Other research claims that financial literacy does not always lead to good financial decision making (Alsemgeest, 2015). According to Alsemgeest (2015), just because one performs well on a financial literacy test, does not necessarily equate to better financial management decisions. Willis (2011) found there are other factors that need to be considered when one is making a financial decision including personality, emotions, and psychology, all of which can give someone predispositions with financial decision making. Willis compared a predisposition of emotional discomfort one may feel to alleviate hunger, which would be to eat. The same can be true with one that is financially literate in that they may have learned how to make better decisions, but their predisposed biases can still overpower rational decision making (Willis, 2011).

Financial Literacy Importance for Entrepreneurship

Financial literacy is beneficial to an entrepreneur and to individuals. Research has shown that financially literate entrepreneurs can manage their businesses more proficiently (Anshika, 2022), minimize financial risks (Vidovicova, 2021), and evolve into better chances of success (Usama & Wan Yusoff, 2018). Furthermore, financial literacy has been found to be an essential skill set that has a positive association to selfemployment (Struckell et al., 2022) and is considered one of the most important attributes that contribute to entrepreneurial tenability (Ali et al., 2018). Some of the skills noted by Ali et al. (2018) include purchasing, allocating, and understanding accounting, costing, and budgeting. Although financial literacy is an important skillset for an entrepreneur, research has indicated there are other skills that are just as or more important (Jardim, 2021). Jardim (2021) conducted a book review to identify the economic, social, and cultural competencies that entrepreneurs should possess. Aside from economic skills, Jardim revealed that effective communication skills (e.g., verbal, digital), creativity, and networking to be among some of the most important soft skills an entrepreneur should possess. Huang et al. (2021) further reiterated the importance of communication skills, especially when pitching to investors. Huang et al. found that communication styles of men and women entrepreneurs differ in that men use more abstract language whereas women use more concrete language, which can be the cause of men being approved for funding more so than women. However, Balachandra et al. (2021) disputed that claim and revealed that although pitching to potential investors is a masculine domain, research has found that women entrepreneurs, when pitching an idea for funding, traditionally use the same language as men to a successful degree. Although many other skills are needed to be successful in entrepreneurship, most of the research points to financial literacy as a core element to establish, grow, and run a tenable business.

Financial Literacy Gender Gaps

A gender gap in financial literacy exists in addition to the gender gap in entrepreneurship based on global and national studies that have found that women are less financially literate than men (Goyal & Kumar, 2021; Lusardi & Mitchell, 2007; Milken Institute, 2021). To combat the financial literacy gender gaps, private and governmental entities have created policies and programs to increase women entrepreneurs' access to financial capital, training, and support. In 2018, the U.S. Department of State established a program called Providing Opportunities for Women's Economic Rise, which aimed to support women's economic participation domestically and globally (Ehdaie & Spring, 2022). Additionally, the SBA (n.d.a) has many resources available to assist women entrepreneurs with funding opportunities at various stages of a business. Gender gaps in entrepreneurship continue to exist indicating that, potentially, these programs and policies developed to support women entrepreneurship allude to perceived deficits in women entrepreneurs rather than focusing on

the systemic gender inequalities that have plagued the nation for centuries

(Coleman et al., 2019). As a result, the programs and policies implemented

have not addressed the gaps in women entrepreneurs' abilities to establish,

operate, and grow a business.

In addition to the gender gaps for existing entrepreneurs, there is also

evidence that gender gaps exist in students wishing to enter the field of

entrepreneurship (Dilli & Westerhuis, 2018). Dilli and Westerhuis (2018)

identified a gender gap in science education, which was found to be

negatively correlated with entrepreneurial activity in knowledge-intensive

sectors. Therefore, it has been suggested, through an examination of

textbooks, syllabi, and curriculums, educators need to design more inclusive

teaching experiences for those wishing to enter the field of entrepreneurship

(C. Elliott et al., 2021).

Although there is strong evidence of a gender gap in financial literacy

and entrepreneurship (Goyal & Kumar, 2021; Lusardi, 2019; Milken

Institute, 2021), most of the results are based on quantitative results that use

Likert-scale measurements, selfassessments, and questions based on the *Big*

Three questionnaire test developed by

Lusardi and Mitchell (2007).

Financial Literacy Measurements

Most studies that are conducted on financial literacy skills use what is

known as the gold standard of measurement, developed by Lusardi and

Mitchell (2007), and was first introduced to measure one's readiness for retirement. The measurement tool contained what became known as the *Big Three*, which indicated there are three fundamental concepts to financial literacy: (a) numeracy skills, (b) understanding inflation, and (c) understanding risk diversification (Lusardi, 2019). The *Big Three* is still used today for journals, policymaking, and education, with expansions to include financial attitudes and behaviors, all aimed at increasing one's ability to make better financial decisions, known as the *Big Five* (Lusardi et al., 2021; Nicolini & Haupt, 2019; Skagerlund et al., 2018). The existing problem highlighted by many is that although the *Big Three* or the updated *Big Five* questionnaire test (i.e., earn, spend, save and invest, borrow, and protect) are great foundational tools, entrepreneurs need to better understand the financial literacy of segmented groups rather than having the entire population rated as a whole (Nicolini & Haupt, 2019). Other critics of financial literacy measurements indicate the wording on financial literacy tests can be confusing, resulting in incorrect responses and not including weighted scores (Ouachani et al., 2021). Furthermore, Ouachani et al. (2021) highlighted that financial literacy testing uses two forms of measurement: (a) objective and (b) subjective. Objective financial literacy assessments focus on knowledge and skills, and subjective assessments focus on an individual's selfconfidence (Ouachani et al., 2021). This makes it more difficult to determine levels of financial literacy as a universal concept. Additionally, Gignac and Ooi (2022) recommended that researchers use a minimum of 13 to 15 questions, rather than the three to five questions that are typically comprised of the *Big Three* and the *Big Five* questionnaire tests to mitigate measurement errors.

Financial Literacy and Microenterprises

As the book review has indicated, financial literacy is of the utmost importance in any entrepreneurial endeavor, regardless of size. Although there is scarce evidence of the financial needs of microenterprises, it has been found that microenterprises have a lower level of financial literacy. Also, more resources are needed for this group. A microenterprise typically operates as a sole proprietor; therefore, the owner must juggle multiple responsibilities (Gross, 2022). Additionally, according to an online survey with approximately 1,200 pre recruited small businesses, conducted by Bank of America (2024) to assess business and economic outcomes, supported the time constraint of women entrepreneurs, Bank of America (2024) report indicated that 34% of women business owners had caregiving responsibilities in addition to running their business, versus 23% of men business owners.

However, the need for financial literacy skills for the microenterprise could be determined to be more important because research (McKay, 2014) indicated that microenterprises only had enough funds to sustain their business for 1 month. The OECD (2022) and its International Network on Financial Education established a framework for on the core competencies that small businesses should have knowledge of and include choice and use of financial services, financial and business management planning, risk and insurance, and financial landscape. Under each core competency, the information is further broken down by specific skills and behaviors one should have to own a business (OECD, 2022). Some of the skills recommended include keeping track of revenue, payments, and deposits, inventory, cash flow, preparation of financial documents, and budgeting.

Because women microenterprises primarily operate as a sole proprietor, they need to juggle tasks (Gross, 2022). The focus cannot only be on selling a product or service. The owner must also act as the chief financial officer to ensure there are enough funds available to keep the business growing. Because it has been documented that microenterprises do not have enough funds to operate for more than a month, financial literacy skills are a necessity to keep this particular type of small business operational to contribute to the economy. With time being a constraint for microenterprises, Aburizaizah and Albaiz (2021) have found that nano learning trainings, which are short tutorials typically less than 2 minutes long without an instructor, are an effective tool, enabling content to be absorbed much easier. Also, it accommodates those with busy schedules. Another form of training are microlearning tools, which are a bit longer than nano learning tools, which last 5 to 15 minutes. The results, thus far, have shown that through repetition, microlearning can contribute to knowledge building, by taking shortterm memory and transferring it into long-term memory (Aburizaizah & Albaiz, 2021). However, there are downsides to nano and microlearning in that information is disseminated in small bites on a specific topic and it does not lend itself to an entire subject, which would require more time (Pritchard,

2017). Although this form of learning is not intended to replace formal courses that cover a variety of topics, it can provide quick information to make decisions.

Fintech

The widespread use of financial technical tools (fintech) is making its popularity soar, with 80% of consumers using some form of fintech to manage their finances in 2022, a jump from 58% in 2020 (Trificana, 2023). Fintech are tools that use apps, software or technology that enable businesses and consumers to digitally manage their finances to gain insights. Some examples of fintech tools include online banking, crowdfunding modeling, bill paying, and peer-to-peer lending (Sharma et al., 2023).

However, there are mixed results on how fintech tools contribute to financial literacy.

According to a report authored by H. Davis and Hasler (2021) through the Global Financial Literacy Excellence Center, researchers conducted an experiment with students using fintech tools and Microsoft Excel for various financial exercises. H. Davis and Hasler (2021) concluded that 1 month after the experiment, 66% of the participants who used the fintech tools changed their budgeting habits for the better, compared to 32% of the respondents that used Microsoft Excel. However, the same report also indicated there were no significant improvements in answering the three fundamental questions that measure financial knowledge: (a) interest compounding, (b) inflation, and (c) risk diversification (H. Davis & Hasler, 2021). Accordingly, research by

Koskelainen et al. (2023) indicated the traditional use of financial literacy and capabilities have been digitally transformed and the use of fintech has benefits and downsides that should be incorporated into curriculums on financial literacy teaching. A report by the Harris Poll Fintech Report (2022) indicated U.S. citizens are feeling better about their financial situation due to the advent of fintech (Plaid.com, 2022); however, data from the Federal Reserve Bank of New York (2023) reported otherwise. Debt balances have risen from the first quarter of 2023 to the second quarter of 2023 by 0.1%, credit card balances have increased by 4.6% in the same quarter, and bankruptcy notations on credit reports have also risen from the first quarter to the second quarter (Federal Reserve Bank of New York, 2023). This trend seems to reveal that although U.S. citizens are paying more attention to their finances, it does not lend itself to an increase in financial literacy.

Entrepreneurs who incorporate some form of fintech into their businesses have positive impacts including improved efficiency, growth, and financial performance; flexibility for women entrepreneurs; and assists with overcoming financial stress (Sharma et al., 2023). Although adoption rates of fintech are not as high as the individual level, small and medium enterprises are anticipated to be the next target of growth for fintech companies, with an estimated market value of $285 billion by 2030 (Giuggioli & Pellegrini, 2023). The uses of fintech by entrepreneurs come in the form of digital payment services, payroll services, and financial statement generation. All these services help to expedite business operations and monitor the health of a company, which has become much more vital since the COVID-19

pandemic (Mullins, 2020).

With the adoption rates of fintech at the individual level and predicted

adoption by SBOs, the U.S. continues to struggle with financial literacy

skills, ranking 14th worldwide (Faulkner, 2022). Many governments, private,

and nonprofit institutions provide financial resources and support to women

entrepreneurs, such as the NAWBO

(n.d.a), SBA (2023a), Goldman Sach's 10,000 Women Initiative (2023), and
Wells Fargo

(n.d.). The U.S. government has spent over $10 billion to support and

empower women entrepreneurship between 2021 to 2022 through loan and

support programs (The White House, 2023). The ease of use with the

introduction of fintech has its advantages to consumers and businesses.

However, the results in the applications to improve financial literacy skills

are still unknown.

Summary

The book review discusses many contrary views about women in

entrepreneurship. The review began with how feminist theories have evolved

from looking at sexual orientation and positioning the women entrepreneur as

less adequate than men. However, the feminist poststructural lens, which was

used in this study as the foundational theory, posits that gender is socially

structured and can be deconstructed, which can hopefully begin a trend of

looking at entrepreneurship neither through gender nor sex but rather, just as entrepreneurship. The book review also examined how entrepreneurship and small business definitions have evolved and how they are used interchangeably through various organizations and government institutions. The characteristics of entrepreneurs have also been examined in the book review, and although there are many differences, there is evidence that some of the characteristics carry over into entrepreneurship, regardless of gender. The book review also examined the various definitions of financial literacy, the importance of it for individuals and entrepreneurs, and the gender gaps that continue to persist in entrepreneurship, even in times of crises. Finally, the book review examined the use of fintech in entrepreneurial endeavors to determine whether the technology may help or hinder the gender gap in entrepreneurship.

Chapter 3, Methodology, discusses in detail the methodology and research design that was used for the study. Chapter 3 also includes how the data were collected, defines the participants of the study, and explains how they were accessed and recruited. Ethical considerations were undertaken, which was to ensure privacy and confidentiality of participants. There is a detailed section on how the data were analyzed, followed by limitations and delimitations of the study, and how the researcher set aside any biases.

CHAPTER 3: METHODOLOGY

The focus of this qualitative study was to explore the meaning of financial literacy from the perspective of women microentrepreneurs that have been running a business in the Pacific Northwest that has been operational for at least 5 or more years, beginning in or before 2019 to March 14, 2020 (before); March 15, 2020, to May 31, 2021 (during); and June 1, 2021, and thereafter (post COVID-19) as that is when the last states in the Pacific Northwest officially reopened (Washington Governor Jay Inslee, 2021). The researcher interviewed 22 microentrepreneurs to better understand how financial literacy helps or hinders the tenability of their business. Conducting the study using a qualitative methodology to identify financial literacy skills has been encouraged by several authors because the most commonly known research approach to determine someone's level of financial literacy is using quantitative measurements. The quantitative measurements that are used typically ask questions about compound interest rates, mortgage interest, bond prices, rates of return, and risk diversification and have resulted in findings that deem women are less financially literate than men (Lusardi et al. 2021; Nicolini & Haupt, 2019; Skagerlund et al., 2018). This result can be a contributing factor to the lack of women's entrepreneurship tenability. Therefore, a qualitative and phenomenological approach was used to reduce the use of statistical measurements and attempt to find an answer through the lived experience of participants.

In Chapter 3, the research methodology used for this study is thoroughly identified, explained, and justified. The research design contains the information required to support the use of a phenomenological research design. Along with the methodology and design, the instrument that was used to carry out the research is explained along with how the data were collected and how trustworthiness was achieved. There is a section on participants, providing a description of who they are, how they were selected, sampling methodology, and sample size. The participant section addressed the ethical considerations that were undertaken to protect the identity of the participants. Following that is a section on how the data were analyzed, including the use of software and techniques used to create categories and themes. Finally, limitations and delimitations of the study are identified and the steps taken to mitigate them are included.

The research questions (RQs) that guided the study included searching for answers to better understand what is deemed to be important for women microentrepreneurs to run a tenable business through the use of financial literacy skills. The questions for the research can assist other entrepreneurs, policymakers, academics, and program developers to better understand what programs and policies should focus on to support women entrepreneurship.

RQ1: What are women entrepreneurs' perceptions of the impact on their business through the lens of their current financial literacy?

RQ2: How do women entrepreneurs acquire the financial skills used in their business?

RQ3: What are the financial approaches, strategies, and challenges, if any, faced by women entrepreneurs?

Research Method

The research method for the study used a qualitative methodology. Women entrepreneurship and financial literacy skills have been researched extensively, primarily through the quantitative methodology and the results have indicated that women entrepreneurs are less financially literate than men (Lusardi et al., 2021; Nicolini & Haupt, 2019; Skagerlund et al., 2018). Therefore, the chosen methodology used a qualitative approach that sought to gain a better understanding of how financial literacy is defined by women microentrepreneurs and how they use the skills identified to develop strategies to operate a tenable business, especially through the COVID-19 pandemic. At its core, qualitative research enables resarchers to explore a phenomenon that is being studied in its natural setting through the use of face-to-face and one-on-one interviews with participants (Creswell & Creswell, 2018). The qualitative methodology infuses *how* and *why* questions into the interview process, rather than statisical methods, such as close-ended questions that are administered through surveys (Patton, 2015). The goal of the research was to explore the experiences of the participants and move away from statistical analysis that uses close-ended questions. Therefore, examining the topic from a qualitative methodology provided illuminating meanings from the participants being interviewed.

Other research methods were ruled out as not being the best fit for the study. Quantitative research uses predetermined questions that are close-ended and typically administered through surveys and are analyzed through statistical analysis and interpretation (Patton, 2015). Because the topic of women entrepreneurship and financial literacy has been oversaturated in the book, quantitative methodology was not used, as it would end up being a redundant process of what is already known. Although the quantitative methodology can provide insight to a larger population and increase generalizability, the qualitative methodology contributes to a more meaningful and indepth understanding of what is being studied and can be transferred and applied to other contexts or groups (Patton, 2015).

The mixed method approach uses a combination of quantitative and qualitative measures (Patton, 2015). The use of predetermined and emerging questions are infused with one another, as are the use of open and close ended questions (Creswell & Creswell, 2018). The mixed method approach also uses several forms of data collection and analysis. The exploratory, sequential mixed methodology begins with quantitative research, which is then analyzed. Based on the results of the quantitative data, researchers then expand upon the findings with qualitative data (Creswell & Creswell, 2018). The mixed method approach was not chosen for the study because of its inherent quantitative characteristics. As mentioned previously, the foundation of the study was to move away from quantitative measurements that have already been established.

Research Design

According to Creswell and Creswell (2018), there are five designs to the qualitative methodology of research: (a) narrative, (b) phenomenological, (c) grounded theory, (d) ethnography, and (e) case studies. Each design aims to explore and understand a phenomenon in an individual or group in a nonnumerical approach. However, emergent experiences are captured differently with each design. The narrative design seeks to tell a historical story about the lived experience of those being studied (Creswell & Creswell, 2018). Because the researcher did not want a historical perspective, the narrative design was deemed inappropriate for the study. Ethnography seeks to study human groups and how their actions form and maintain a culture and uses rituals, ceremonies, and artifacts as areas of observation (Moustakas, 1994; O'Neill et al., 2023). The researcher did not view women entrepreneurs as a culture; therefore, this design was rejected. Grounded theory is used when a new theory is generated from the research and data collection processes (Moustakas, 1994; Thornberg et al., 2023). Because a theory had been identified and the researcher did not seek to create a new theory, grounded theory was also rejected as a research design. Case studies are used when researchers seek to explore and investigate a single event over time (Creswell & Creswell, 2018). The aim of the study was not to focus on a single event, as it can minimize the lived experiences of women entrepreneurs. Therefore, case studies were also rejected as a research design.

As such, the phenomenological approach was deemed as the most appropriate design for the study.

The research design followed a phenomenological approach to be able to obtain the answers to the research questions through the lived experience of the participants. The phenomenological research design is rooted in philosophy and aims to incorporate consciousness, knowledge, and the worldview of the phenomenon taking place using the first-person lived experiences of individuals (Suddick et al., 2020; Vagle, 2018). The origins of phenomenology date back to writings from Greek philosopher Aristotle; however, Husserl has been credited as the founder of phenomenology, which takes on a descriptive approach to studying the lived experiences of individuals (Marshall & Rossman, 2016; Qutoshi, 2018). Later writings from Heidegger viewed phenomenology from a heuristic perspective, which is interpretive (Horrigan-Kelly et al., 2016). Others view heuristics as a simpler and quicker way of gaining answers to difficult questions (Hjeij & Vilks, 2023; Nouri & AhmadiKafeshani, 2020). The researcher used heuristic phenomenology, which was originally designed to interpret biblical texts; however, Heidegger, expanded hermeneutics into a "theory of understanding [and] retained its focus on interpretation, but expanded it to focus on philosophical and ontological matters" (as cited in Vagle, 2018, p. 15). With heuristic research, the goal is to not read and interpret textual content that comes from interviews. According to Vagle (2018), using hermeneutics and phenomenology together moves away from an epistemological interest (to know) and moves toward ontological (to be) interest. Therefore, the most suitable design for this study was the phenomenological approach combined with heuristics to go beyond descriptive analysis of the textual content from interviews into a deeper understanding of the content.

Conceptual Framework

A conceptual framework shows the relationship between concepts and their impact on the phenomenon being investigated. A conceptual framework intends to clarify, explain, and justify methodological decisions (Luft et al., 2022). With a conceptual framework, researchers position their philosophical worldviews that translate the research approach into perspective. Because this study used a phenomenological approach, whereby data were collected and analyzed from one-on-one interviews with participants, the worldview selected was ontological, which is concerned with the nature of being. Ontology was selected over epistemology, which focuses on the nature of knowing (Ataro, 2020). The nature of being was considered the most suitable for this study as it is the belief that there can be multiple realities and the only way to uncover one reality is through an individual or group one is seeking an answer from (Feyisa, 2022). This study sought to uncover the reality of how women microentrepreneurs defined financial literacy and thus, resulted in a new way of being, which can influence social change in the field of entrepreneurship.

Data Collection

Qualitative research involves observations and inquiry, making the primary instrument the researcher (Creswell & Creswell, 2018; Patton, 2015). The data were obtained through individual face-to-face interviews, via video and audio conferencing, using semi-structured questions (see Appendix A) and guided the interview to answer the research questions. Patton (2015) emphasized the importance of having the researcher immerse themselves in the interview process by practicing openness, understanding, empathy, confidentiality, and mindfulness, to develop a rapport with participants. In doing so, this can elevate the credibility of the results and establish trustworthiness (Patton, 2015). The first semi-structured question of the interviews began with a prompt for the participants to talk about their business. This was followed by open-ended questions to solicit answers to the second research question. Examples of open-ended questions included asking participants to describe what they deemed as the most important and then least important financial skill needed for a business owner and why. The third and final research question included questions about the financial strategies microentrepreneurs had used to run a tenable business. The objective was to ask questions using *how* and *what* questions because it enabled flexibility with emerging themes, and they solicit more in-depth responses instead of questions that prompt yes, no, or one-word answers (Creswell & Creswell, 2018). Additionally, Patton (2015) and others (Castillo-Montoya, 2016) recommend avoiding *why* questions, as they can lead to dead-end answers

(Patton, 2015) and can be perceived as judgmental (CastilloMontoya, 2016). Rather, the use of *what* should be used in its place. The interviews concluded with a closing statement by the researcher that enabled participants to ask any questions or for the researcher to make any clarifying comments.

To capture the essence of a lived experience of women microentrepreneurs, data collection took form by interviewing participants via video and audio conferencing using the Zoom platform (Zoom, n.d.), which enabled the researcher to develop a worldview of the phenomenon under study (Creswell & Creswell, 2018; Vagle, 2018). For this research study, the focus was on women microentrepreneurs and their understanding of financial literacy. Capturing this type of data must be carefully established to not necessarily solicit responses, rather, it was used to capture the meaning of the experience of the participants (Byrne, 2022). An interview protocol, suggested by Creswell and Creswell (2018), was implemented for the study. The protocol included a log of information maintained by the researcher at each interview and was comprised of information that captured demographic data, such as name, date, type of business, site location, and a unique identifier for each interview. The names with associated identifiers have been maintained confidentially to protect the identity of the participants by using pseudonyms.

The way interview questions are designed is a vital part of setting up the research to elicit responses that align with the study and must be carefully articulated, defined, and refined (Patton, 2015). For the study, the goal was to develop semi-structured, openended questions in a way that made the questions more inquiry-based and conversational, rather than using quantitative analyses of experiments, comparisons, or correlations (Vagle, 2018). This entailed ensuring the semi-structured questions that were used during the interview process did not mimic the actual research questions, rather, they were designed in a way that promoted conversational type approaches and prompts, which was found to be beneficial if the conversation begins going off key (Brinkmann, 2022). To elicit more conversational type questions, researchers should use introductory, transition, key, and closing questions (Castillo-Montoya, 2016). Therefore, the questions were designed to eliminate jargon and used supportive everyday conversational themes that were knowledgeable to the participants. As an example, asking participants how they defined financial literacy was too broad of a question and might be intimidating. Rather, the researcher first probed the participants about their business. It was also important to limit the questions and ask one at a time, which eliminated interrupting the participants and using nods to affirm comprehension (Brinkmann, 2022).

When conducting interviews, there were many factors that were taken into consideration. The interviews began with an introduction by the researcher and an icebreaker, as recommended by Creswell and Creswell (2018) to further gain trust and comfort. The introduction was done in a manner that made participants feel comfortable and aware of what they had agreed to. Once the introduction was made, participants were asked to acknowledge and consent to audio recording. Throughout the interview, the researcher also relied on symbols and prompts to include nonverbal gestures, such as tone of voice, hesitation, and pauses. Therefore, listening to what was said or not said through voices and gestures was just as crucial, which has contributed to enhance women's entrepreneurial identities (Surangi, 2022). The researcher anticipated there would be one interview per participant and if there was a need for clarification, a second interview would have been conducted. However, there was no need for clarification, which resulted in one interview per participant. The main goal of the interviews was to allow responses to occur in their natural setting and allow for experiences, emotions, and opinions of the phenomenon's meaning to emerge (Vagle, 2018).

Audio Recording

A common method for recording in-person or video face-to-face interviews in phenomenological research is using audio devices (Creswell & Creswell, 2018). Researchers must ensure the confidentiality of the participants and the recording device usage is communicated to the participants. Researchers also should have two sources of recording devices in case one method fails (Creswell & Creswell, 2018). Zoom (n.d.) has an audio component to their software, which was used and as a back-up, conversations were being recorded on the researcher's iPhone. Audio recordings served two purposes: (a) it increased the face-to-face, conversational interaction between the researcher and participant; and (b) it provided a way to replay the interview for the analysis portion of the study. Sometimes audio recording interviews can cause anxiety or false information when used in qualitative interviewing (McMullin, 2023). The topic of

financial literacy with women entrepreneurship can make participants feel

intimidated because there is so much research available placing women at a

disadvantage on the topic (Lusardi et al. 2021; Nicolini & Haupt, 2019;

Skagerlund et al., 2018) therefore, the researcher made every effort to

celebrate the participants' accomplishments. Additionally, Rutakumwa et al.

(2020) has found that although audio recording can elicit fear in participants,

they found that when it is omitted (nonaudio recording) researchers may

leave out valuable details and begin to make assumptions based on their

knowledge. Therefore, to maintain the integrity of the interviews, audio

recordings were used. Making all intentions clear from the onset of the

interview was the strategy that was used to eliminate the potential of false or

dishonest information due to the anxiety of being audio recorded.

Video Recording

Videoconferencing software (i.e., Zoom) was used for the interviews,

which has been found to be a more practical approach to qualitative research,

as it makes it convenient and flexible for participants and reduces travel

expenses for the researcher (Khan & MacEachen, 2022). One of the

downsides of video recording can be connectivity issues and anxiety over the

learning curves that may occur due to the use of technology (Merriam &

Tisdell, 2016). However, Keen et al. (2022) found that video conferencing

does not compromise quality, level of rapport, and methodological rigor. For

the convenience of the participants, all interviews were conducted via video recording; however, only the audio was used for data analysis. As indicated by Merriam and Tisdell (2016), issues with quality did occur, with some interviews getting bogged down due to bandwidth issues, causing audio and video to become blurred. Therefore, the researcher turned off the video component in Zoom at times to increase the bandwidth of audio quality, which is recommended by Zoom (2021). This action did improve audio communications. Thus, only the audio portion of the interviews were used for data analysis. Once interviews concluded, the audio file was downloaded and saved to an external hard drive and encrypted, to ensure confidentiality and privacy of the participants and the video portion of the interview files were discarded. The researcher found that using only the audio portion of the interviews did not compromise the integrity of the interviews in any way, because the audio transcripts were recorded verbatim and captured pauses and *umms*. Additionally, the researcher made notes on a piece of paper during the interviews. The paper included semi-structured interview questions with enough space in between each question to document any noteworthy gestures or comments as the interviews took place.

Once the participants agreed to take part in the study, all efforts were made to contact the participants prior to the interviews through email to fully explain the intentions, format, and technical specifications of the study. Participants were advised that there could be no right or wrong answers, no quantitative testing was administered, and the interviews would be audio recorded. During the initial engagement, participants were also notified of the potential length of the interview (i.e., 60 to 90 minutes), and that it was going to be audio recorded. Participants were also informed that an additional interview may be necessary, and they would be able to review the interview notes, once they were transcribed. The initial engagement period is especially important because it can help to alleviate any anxieties or fears participants may have, which can cause disengagement, dishonesty, and intimidation (Creswell & Creswell, 2018; McMullin, 2023). All the information was saved to City University of Seattle's encrypted password protected storage. If there was any documentation shared with the researcher during interviews, that information would have been scanned, uploaded, and followed the same protocol as the researcher's data; however, there was no additional information gathered.

Once the interviews were completed, the researcher used a closing speech to take the opportunity to thank the participants and to also provide them with the opportunity to ask questions. Although the questions asked at the end of the interview are not part of the research questions, they can elicit additional information (Sowicz et al., 2019). In the bibliographic study conducted by Sowicz et al. (2019), 81% of respondents indicated that they always use closing questions in their research for several reasons. Some respondents stated that closing questions add to the interview data, they can reveal new areas of exploration, or they can be used to modify interview guides. Additionally, some respondents stated the use of closing comments and questions are not used in data analysis; rather, they are used as a prompt to signal the end of the interview or clarify responses (Sowicz et al., 2019).

The closing statement did not garner additional information; however, it did provide a transition to the closing of the interview and gave the participants an opportunity to have a voice in the study and an opportunity for the researcher to thank the participants for their time.

Participants

Regardless of the research methodology, quantitative or qualitative, participants are a subset of people that have some commonality in which researchers seek knowledge from (Chadwick, 2017). The target population for this study was women microentrepreneurs that owned and operated a business in the Pacific Northwest and have less than 5 employees. If the microentrepreneur had employees, the employees were not interviewed for the study, as the primary focus was on the lived experience of the women microentrepreneur. Each participant was a business owner, registered with their respective Department of State as an active business. The participants owned a business from 2019 or prior through 2024. These dates were specifically chosen as they coincide with the COVID-19 pandemic. In the region of the Pacific Northwest, there are 10,490 women microenterprises that have zero employees and an additional 35,778 businesses that have one to four employees (Small Business Administration [SBA], 2023h).

Therefore, the entire population was 46,268 businesses.

Participant Search

The researcher used several databases and associations to identify potential candidates for the study. The databases included the SBA,

Department of States for each respective state, and the National Association of Women Business Owners. The researcher also used the social media platform LinkedIn to identify potential participants. The researcher developed a potential participant list in Microsoft Excel, which has been deemed an efficient way of keeping track of data that is being collected (Ose, 2016). Once potential participants were identified, they were sent an invitation to participate in the study via email. Any participant that accepted the initial invitation was then provided with a consent form to participate in the study. The information gathered on the consent form provided participants with the purpose of the study, researcher information and university affiliation, along with a confidentiality clause that reaffirmed the participant's willingness to participate in the study. Upon return of the consent forms, interviews were scheduled by the researcher and all efforts were made to ensure the participants' availability were met.

Sampling Methodology

The emphasis of qualitative research is not the number of participants, rather, it seeks to minimize the number of participants to capture the lived experiences of a selected few through in-depth interviews (Patton, 2015). The participant pool was narrowed by applying two criteria: (a) geographical location limited to the Pacific

Northwest (i.e., Washington, Oregon, Idaho, and Montana) and (b) women entrepreneurs that have less than 5 employees. For easy reference, Table 3.1 is a replication of Table 1.1, which provides a breakdown of women-owned

businesses in the Pacific Northwest.

It is repeated in the table for convenience for the reader.

Table 3.1

*Women-Owned Businesses in the Pacific Northwest by State With 0
Employees and Less Than 5 Employees*

State	0 employees	1 to 4 employees	Total
Idaho	1,492	3,856	5,348
Montana	1,028	3,904	4,932
Oregon	3,063	10,814	13,877
Washington	4,907	17,204	22,111
Total	10,490	35,778	46,268

Note. The data were pulled from the National Center for Science and
Engineering

Statistics within the National Science Foundation and the U.S. Census Bureau
(2021).

A further delineation was made to the participant pool to target women

microentrepreneurs that have been in business prior to 2019 and through

2024. Because of the COVID-19 pandemic, many businesses were forced to

shut down (Decker & Haltiwanger, 2022), and therefore, businesses that

temporarily ceased operations due to mandatory shutdowns were still

considered for the study. Purposeful and snowball sampling were used to

recruit participants.

Purposeful Sampling

There are a variety of techniques to select participants for a study, and the type of study being undertaken determines the sampling technique. In qualitative research, the goal is to gain depth, not breadth from participants (Patton, 2015); thus, the selection of participants was conducted through purposeful sampling. In purposeful sampling, also known as judgment sampling, the researcher makes a deliberate effort to select participants based on the qualities they possess, not the easy access they may offer (Etikan et al., 2016; Patton, 2015).

Snowball Sampling

Because the participants selected are very small, the researcher also instituted a secondary sampling methodology; snowball sampling, also known as chain or networking sampling (Patton, 2015). Snowball sampling is a process whereby the researcher identified others that might be familiar with the topic of research through potential participants and then asked them if they knew of anyone else that might want to participate in the study. Snowball sampling was also a way for the researcher to collect any relevant information that could have provided the researcher with additional participants such as organizations and associations. Therefore, at the end of each interview, the researcher asked the participants if they knew of anyone fitting the criteria that might be interested in partaking in the study. Snowball sampling did not result in any new participants.

Recruitment of Participants

The process of recruiting participants involved identifying, targeting, and enlisting potential participants, which was then followed by providing potential participants with information about the study to seek interest in participating (Manohar et al., 2018). When recruiting, the researcher ensured the goals of selecting qualified candidates were performed ethically. Additionally, the researcher was cognizant of the potential fears that participants may have had over the confidentiality of their information. Recruitment for participants was conducted in three ways: (a) personal network, (b) organizations and associations, and (c) online through social media.

Personal Network

The researcher had a vast personal network of participants who met the criteria of the study. As part of the personal network initiative, snowball sampling was incorporated by asking known contacts for their knowledge of anyone who might be interested in participating in the study. Those who met the criteria were contacted via email in the same manner as participants that were selected via purposeful sampling. The personal network initiative resulted in two participants and followed the same protocol of signing a consent form.

Organizations and Associations

There are a plethora of organizations and associations specifically for women entrepreneurs such as the SBA, Department of States, the National

Association of Women Business Owners, and local organizational chapters. Most of the data from these resources supplied sufficient data to be able to create filters that met the criteria for the study. The U.S. Census Bureau (2022), through the Annual Business Survey report provided users a way to filter the data on gender, and geographical location. Data from the 2021 Annual Business Survey report were downloaded to include the required criteria. Once potential participants were identified, the researcher then used resources such as LinkedIn to obtain email addresses, which was the first form of communication used for recruitment.

Online

Because many people conduct business online, either for personal or professional reasons, the researcher created an online recruitment campaign. There was an ad placed on LinkedIn, a professional networking site. The ad contained information about the study and had a call-to-action section so that any willing potential participants were able to contact the researcher via their institutional or personal email address. This initiative resulted in two participants.

Sample Size

Most scholars recommend in-depth interviews of 5 to 25 participants (Dworkin, 2012; Marshall & Rossman, 2016). Lincoln and Guba (1985) emphasized the sample size should be enough until data saturation has been accomplished, which is when interviews do not yield any new information. Therefore, the sample size was based on the information gained from the interviews. When the researcher began to hear the same, or redundant, information, and there was no new knowledge gained, the researcher determined that data saturation had been accomplished. Upon using all forms of recruitment possibilities mentioned previously, 22 consent forms were obtained, and 22 interviews were conducted.

Data Analysis Methods

Through the combination of researcher notes and the transcribed interviews, the data analysis followed the hierarchical approach used in qualitative research, which is preparing the raw data to be analyzed. Next, data are transcribed, read, coded, placed into themes, and then interpreted into comprehensive findings (Creswell & Creswell, 2018). Creswell and Creswell's (2018) seven-step process was used for data analysis in this study. The steps outlined by Creswell and Creswell (2018) include (a) organizing and preparing the data, (b) reading and looking at all the data, (c) coding the data, (d) developing categories, (e) developing descriptions, (f) developing themes, and finally, (g) interpreting the meaning of the data. In addition to the seven-step process, establishing trustworthiness of the data was of the utmost importance because qualitative research has endured much scrutiny over its trustworthiness compared to quantitative research (Morse et al., 2022). The goal of establishing trustworthiness is to ensure that the research is conducted ethically, precisely, consistently, transparently, and meticulously documented (Nowell et al., 2017). Trustworthiness was established through maintaining an audit trail that documented every phase of the process.

Organizing and Preparing the Data

Once the interviews concluded, the researcher took all the data and organized them into individual files that used the pseudonym given to each participant. The data were comprised of researcher notes and audio of the interviews. The interviews, along with notes, were transcribed verbatim and included the capture of nonverbal characteristics, which were captured by hand-written notes by the researcher as the interview was taking place. As an example, while the interviews were underway, the researcher prepared a list of the semi-structured questions, with enough space in between each question, to make any notations such as emphases, pauses, and tone. Hitchcock and Onwuegbuzie (2020) recommended capturing nonverbal gestures such as body movements (i.e., kinesics), silences and pauses (i.e., chronemics), and tone (i.e., paralinguistics), which can potentially add to the interpretation of results.

Looking at the Data

Once the data were transcribed, the researcher underwent a rigorous process of reading through the data. In doing so, the researcher reflected upon the overall meaning of the transcribed data and immersed themselves in the data. Reading and rereading can develop an overarching understanding of the content and provide the researcher with developing codes (Creswell & Creswell, 2018). The transcribed data were formatted in MS Word, using the "wide" margin setting, which is one inch for top and bottom margins and two inches for left and right margins. The transcribed files were printed out and thoughts and ideas were written into the margins to be referenced later. Some of the thoughts and ideas that were written down including gestures that were captured during the interview. For example, using the semi-structured interview questions print-out, the researcher made notations under some of the responses by using a smiley face emoji, to depict happiness. Another example of capturing nonverbal gestures using the semistructured interview questions print-out was using the letter "P" to indicate a pause in between the question that was asked and the response that was given. These gestures were then inserted into the transcribed files that were printed out.

Coding the Data

Coding is the process of taking all the data and breaking it into analytical units, such as words, phrases, or sentences representing a single idea that could potentially represent a category in the margins of the document (Creswell & Creswell, 2018). There were several steps that were undertaken to code the data in the most practical, transparent, and ethical ways possible. To begin the coding process, the transcribed data were printed out and the researcher performed color coding and line-by-line coding, which was the process of reading through each interview and highlighting blocks of text (Creswell & Creswell, 2018) that the researcher felt was relevant. In addition to highlighting blocks of text, the researcher also made comments on each transcribed file that could potentially be used as a category.

Coding was done using predetermined (a priori) and emergent codes that came directly from the participants (in vivo) from the data (Creswell &

Creswell, 2018; V. Elliott, 2018). Using prefigured and emergent coding are typically used in a research project (V. Elliott, 2018). Therefore, the research contained both forms of coding. Some of the a priori codes that were established involved theory and research generated codes. Research has indicated that engaging in the data can be valuable for creating codes (Locke et al., 2020). For this research, the a priori codes included emotions, feelings, challenges, and strategies. Codes are descriptive in nature and were used as an inventory of the data that had been collected. The a priori codes mentioned previously were not intended to be an exhaustive list of a priori codes. However, based on the book, these are commonly used when researching women entrepreneurs from a poststructural feminist lens (Ahl & Marlow, 2012; Cardella et al., 2020).

Developing Categories

Once line-by-line coding was completed, the next step was abstraction, which was taking the codes and developing them into categories (Creswell & Creswell, 2018). Creating categories is, in essence, identifying patterns in the data, whether they were similar, dissimilar, frequent, or sequential. The process of categorizing is classifying the data through reasoning and through the researchers' intuitive senses to determine which data are similar (Lincoln & Guba, 1985). Categorizing is a method that enables a researcher to organize and group similarly coded data into categories or *families* because they share some characteristic. The researcher took to pen and paper and hand-wrote potential categories on individual sheets of paper. Thereafter, the corresponding comments from the line-by-line and color coding were written on the sheet of paper. This was done for every interview.

Many of the categories that were created by the researcher came from semistructured interview questions. For example, the way financial skills were obtained was a semi-structured interview question, which was used as a category. The number of categories suggested is anywhere from 25 to 30 categories, which most researchers find to be a manageable amount (Creswell & Creswell, 2018; Merriam & Tisdell, 2016). To create categories, the researcher used the four guidelines suggested by Lincoln and Guba (1985). The first step was to take note of the number of participants that mentioned something similar to capture frequency in the data. The second step was taking note of who the intended audience of the results might be to determine what was important. The third step included considering categories that are unique, and finally, paying attention to emerging categories that could be out of the scope of the research question but is worth exploring (Lincoln & Guba, 1985; Merriam & Tisdell, 2016). Once the coding and categorizing processes were performed manually, the data were then transferred to a computer-aided qualitative data analysis software program, NVivio V14, which is desribed in more detail in the next section.

Computer-Aided Qualitative Data Analysis Software

In addition to human coding, the researcher used computer-aided qualitative data analysis software (CAQDAS). The software that was used was NVivo, specifically NVivo V14. NVivo is the most used software tool used in qualitative and mixed methods research (Ose, 2016). Ose (2016) pointed out that NVivo is typically used when there is unstructured data that come from interviews, articles, open-ended survey responses, and social media content. Although there are many other CAQDAS tools available, NVivo is privately licensed and not cloud-based for individual users (Lumivero.com, n.d.), which added another layer of confidentiality and rigor to the study (Maher et al., 2018). Once line-by-line coding and categories were established, the researcher recreated the categories in NVivo, and transcribed files were then uploaded into NVivo. Blocks of text that were color coded were moved into the categories. NVivo was not used to create any categories. Rather, it was used as an organizational tool, making it easier to view the blocks of texts under the categories in one place. This aided the researcher in being able to look at a category and view the moved blocks of texts from the audio transcriptions in one place, making it easier to associate categories with responses from participants instead of ruffling through the sheets of paper where coding originally took place. The goal of using a CAQDAS program is to assist the researcher in demonstrating trustworthiness, through consistency, lack of bias, and enough detail for replication (Clarke et al., 2021). Although using NVivo was a repetitive process that was done manually by the researcher, it provided the researcher the opportunity to further immerse themselves in the data. NVivo was not used to interpret any of the data; rather, it was used for organization of the data.

If NVivo V14 was found to not be the best choice or too complicated, the researcher would have explored alternative CAQDAS programs; however, NVivo V14 was suitable for the study. Although CAQDAS tools are not intended to replace the human coding element of qualitative data, it does have some advantages. First, it provides efficiency of coding the data, and enhances the transparency of data analysis. More importantly, CAQDAS tools are used to complement the research process and not replace it (Maher et al., 2018). In this vein, NVivo did assist the researcher with being able to organize the coded data into appropriate categories, which were first performed by hand, making it easier to refer to the data. That was the extent of how the CAQDAS tool was used.

Developing Themes

Themes are invisible impressions and experiences of participants and cannot be seen; rather, the words of the participants were turned into abstract and subtle expressions, patterns, and processes that explained the phenomenon under study. Themes can evolve into nouns, action words, and metaphors. The main goal of creating themes is to provide a conceptual and theoretical level of insight into a phenomenon (Braun & Clarke, 2006; Sundler et al., 2019). The themes that were created came as a result of examining the data and categories repeatedly to find similarities, differences, and repeated subjects and topics. As an example, the researcher examined a category that was recreated in NVivo. When clicking on a category in the software, it displayed all the corresponding coding under that category by participant. Using "Acquisition of Skills" as an example, the researcher clicked on that category and examined all the corresponding codes associated with that category. On a piece of paper, outside of NVivo, the researcher then parceled out any mentions of how participants acquired financial skills. This resulted into the theme of "Support Tools." "Emotions" was another category that turned into more than one theme, as there were emotions of passion of being a business owner, emotions about the topic of finance, and emotions about the COVID-19 pandemic, which all turned into themes. As with coding and categorizing, thematic analysis was an iterative process, and it took many times to identify themes that explain the phenomenon of women entrepreneurship and financial literacy.

To visually represent codes, categories, and themes, word cloud clusters were used. Cluster analysis is the creation of a diagram of relationships (Creswell & Creswell, 2018). To create word clusters, the researcher took hand-written notes from the data analysis and manually counted words that were stated as they related to a category. For example, when the participants were asked about the importance of monitoring their finances, the researcher went to the hand-written notes and listed the responses based on the participants (A through V). Responses included important, critical, vital, moderate to very, really important, and others. The number of times the word important was used was then added up the researcher used a word cloud generator for the visual aspect. An example of a cluster analysis is shown in Figure 3.1. It is designed to illuminate how the data fits together in a visually appealing manner.

Figure 3.1

Systematic Review of Women Entrepreneur Studies

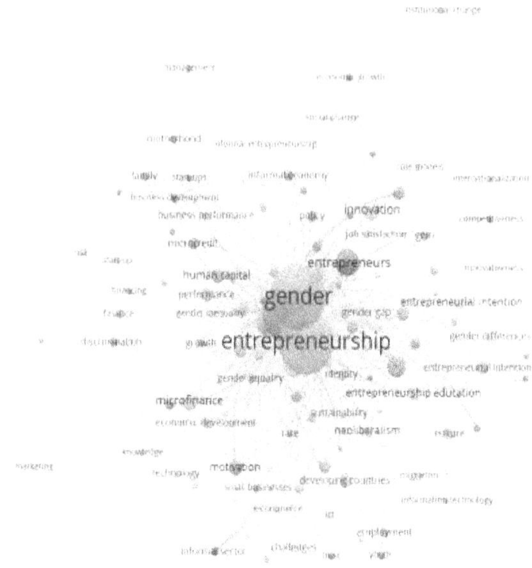

Note. Figure 3.1 is a depiction from a study conducted by Cardella et al. (2020), who outlined research conducted women entrepreneurs from 2006 through 2019. The intended use of this figure is to provide an example of clustering.

Interpretation of Themes

The final step of analyzing the data was interpreting the themes that were derived into meaningful and appropriate interpretations of the participants' words (Creswell & Creswell, 2018; Larsen & Adu, 2022). To interpret the themes, the researcher used direct quotes obtained from the interviews to display connections. The initial line-by-line coding sections of interviews were used to display the mapping of quotes to categories and themes, which can be found in the findings section in Chapter 4. The researcher copied and pasted the direct quotes from the transcribed data files from MS Word.

During the entire research effort, an audit trail was maintained by the researcher to document every process undertaken, ensuring that the findings of the study were the results of the stance of the respondents and were free from research bias, motivation, or interest (Lincoln & Guba, 1985). Merriam and Tisdell (2016) likened the description of an audit trail to that of an accountant maintaining financial records for a company. The records may not be able to be replicated by another company due to different expenses and revenues; however, providing the results of how the entries were made should suffice. Afterall, the objective was to provide meaningful results that can be transferred to others. Transferability, for this study, was attained by providing rich, detailed, and accurate descriptions of the entire study to enable future and current entrepreneurs, policymakers, and academics to use the information for future research.

Limitations and Biases

As indicated in Chapter 2, there were limitations to this study such as interference of biases due to the design approach of audio/video recording of interviews, lack of participants due to the subject matter, and the researcher's background. This section discusses the limitations and biases and techniques that were used to mitigate them.

Conducting qualitative research can interfere with social desirability bias, the desire to interpret research findings to what is socially acceptable (Bergen & Labonte, 2020). Avoiding social desirability bias is especially important when examining a phenomenon through a feminist lens and on the topic of financial literacy, where women have been found to be less knowledgeable (Nicolini & Haupt, 2019). Therefore, a strategy was implemented to look out for and mitigate social desirability bias. The first step was to be on the lookout for characteristics that tend to give way to social desirability bias. For example, paltering can be an indication, as well as nervous facial expressions, and inconsistencies in responses (Bergen & Labonte, 2020). To mitigate social desirability bias, the researcher provided assurance to participants about how anonymity and confidentiality were going to be maintained. Additionally, when necessary, the research used probing if answers were vague, such as, "Can you tell me more about that?" Providing context around the research questions is another strategy that was employed to relieve any of the stress that participants may have been feeling.

In addition to recognizing social desirability bias, the researcher ensured that interviews were conducted in private so that participants did not feel any pressure from external influences. The researcher also established a rapport with the participants to ensure they were fully aware of the purpose of the study and how the results were going to be used.

The study was conducted using a qualitative and phenomenological approach using interviews that were recorded. Most importantly, reinforcements were made to reiterate that there are no right or wrong answers to any of the research questions. Additionally, due to the nature of the topic of financial literacy, participants were notified that statistics were not part of the research.

In qualitative research, there is also the possibility of biases by the researcher. The biases formed by a researcher can include passing judgement onto a participant or inserting preconceptions, which can alter the results of how the research is gathered, interpreted, and presented (Patton, 2015; Thomas & Sohn, 2023). To overcome these obstacles, the researcher used bracketing, also known as epoch, which is setting aside any predispositions, thoughts, assumptions, previous experiences, and beliefs to avoid bias in interviewing (Weatherford & Maitra, 2019), which can increase the rigor of the study. Bracketing took the form of reflexivity, which is a core characteristic of qualitative research (Creswell & Creswell, 2018). Reflexivity is the ability for the researcher to be self-conscious of their role in the research (England, 1994; Patton, 2015). Because the researcher is a woman with a background in the finance industry and experience with entrepreneurship, reflection was critical to set aside biases.

Delimitations

There were boundaries set by the researcher that established delimitations in the study. Any boundaries that were intentionally set by researchers rendered the research not generalizable and transferable to a broader population. The first delimitation was the nature of qualitative research, in that large amounts of participants were not required (Patton, 2015). To mitigate this, the researcher interviewed 22 participants, two above the required minimum number of participants. Secondly, the location of women microentrepreneurs for the study were limited to companies located in the Pacific Northwest, which may not be generalizable to other locations, such as other states across the U.S. Additionally, date parameters of an operational business by a woman microentrepreneur located in the Pacific Northwest was limited to 2019 or prior, through 2024, or still in operation. The date parameters were intentionally selected to examine participants that navigated through the COVID-19 pandemic. Therefore, some findings may not be transferable to other future periods.

Summary

The purpose of Chapter 3 was meant to provide step-by-step guide of the research study to provide transparency and trustworthiness. The topic of the study was to interview women microentrepreneurs and to determine how they use their financial skills to run a tenable business. Because the topic has been researched exhaustively in quantitative research, the chosen methodology was qualitative, and the researcher used a phenomenological research design. When using qualitative and phenomenological procedures, there are certain data collection principles that must be followed to ensure trustworthiness and ethical practices to uphold the validity of study and privacy and confidentiality of participants. To capture the essence of a lived experience of women entrepreneurs the study used semi-structured face-to-face interview questions. An interview protocol was developed to capture data before, during, and after interviews.

Chapter 3 also contained a section on how participants were recruited, the sampling methodology that was used, and a step-by-step guide on how the data were analyzed through organizing, reading, coding, categorizing, theming, and interpreting the data. There are limitations and delimitations to every study, and Chapter 3 provided an outline of them, including biases, which the researcher overcame through social desirability, interview biases, and bracketing. Delimitations were also noted, and due to the nature of qualitative research, the results may not be generalized and transferable to a broader population, because qualitative research uses a sample size that is smaller than quantitative research. There was also a section on how the data were presented in the findings, which used several approaches such as lists, tables, relevant quotes from participants' voices, graphs, and figures. Most importantly, Chapter 3 described in detail how the research was conducted in the most ethical manner possible through member checking, consent forms, and processes.

CHAPTER 4: FINDINGS

The qualitative study explored the meaning, knowledge, acquisition, and use of financial skills of women entrepreneurs that have less than 5 employees, considered microentrepreneurs, in the Pacific Northwest in the U.S. which included Idaho, Montana, Oregon, and Washington states, before, during, and post COVID-19 from the poststructural feminist theory. The poststructural feminist theory posits that acts of discrimination between men and women are not sex-based but rather a result of the social construct, which changes over time (Foss et al., 2019; Lather, 1992). Therefore, the research aimed to contribute to the gap in the book that examines how women entrepreneurs define, acquire, and use their financial literacy skills to run a tenable business and to better understand if they felt they are systemically oppressed from receiving equal treatment due to a lack in financial literacy skills. The research questions (RQs) that guided this study were:

RQ1: What are women entrepreneurs' perceptions of the impact on their business through the lens of their current financial literacy?

RQ2: How do women entrepreneurs acquire the financial skills used in their business?

RQ3: What are the financial approaches, strategies, and challenges, if any, faced by women entrepreneurs?

The study was conducted using a qualitative methodology, which enables researchers to explore phenomena in their natural setting using interviews with participants (Creswell & Creswell, 2018). In doing so, researchers can collect data through multiple sources, such as interviews and observations, which depict the participants' own words. Furthermore, a phenomenological research design was used to obtain answers to questions regarding the financial literacy of women entrepreneurs through their lived experiences. Using a qualitative methodology and phenomenological approach, semi-structured interviews were used to better understand the lived experiences of women-owned microentrepreneurs. The semi-structured interview questions did not mimic the research questions. Rather, the semi-structured interview questions were designed in a way to promote a conversation.

A total of 22 participants were interviewed for the study. To protect the identity of the participants, each was given an alphabetically pseudonym, which refers to the participants as PA, PB, PC, through PV (22 participants). Each interview was conducted via Zoom and the audio and video of the participants were recorded and lasted on average 60 minutes. However, only the oral portion of the transcript was used for data analysis because the internet connection became weak and video was turned off to improve the quality of the voices of the participants. At the end of each interview, participants were supplied with a copy of the transcript to ensure their words have been depicted accurately, to enhance the validity and credibility of the results, which is known as interviewee transcript review (Rowlands, 2021). Rowlands (2021) explained how interviewee transcript review is used as a way to also increase participants' confidence and anonymity, which did not result in any modifications to the original transcripts.

Chapter 4 presents the data obtained from participants through the lens of poststructural feminist theory, which resulted in different perspectives of what constitutes a deficiency in financial literacy skills of women entrepreneurs versus what is essential for them to know. The organization of Chapter 4 begins with demographic information
on the participants including geographical location, business industry, and number of employees. Demographic information is followed by an explanation of how the data were analyzed and the findings of the data analysis.

Participant Selection and Demographics

A total of 202 potential participants were contacted over the course of 2 months to end up with 22 participants. The search for potential participants included searching each state's governmental websites to find businesses that were operational during the date parameters of the study and were listed as active. Although the websites did not provide the number of employees, it was a way to put together a list of potential participants' pool. Once the list was created, techniques were used to acquire participants including visiting the business website, LinkedIn emails, an online ad campaign, Chamber of Commerce, YELP, referrals, personal network, and snowball sampling. Once an email address was obtained, all company data were listed in an Excel spreadsheet that included company name, owner name, address, business start date, industry, year of establishment, email address, and phone number.

Because the number of employees at each participant's business was unknown using this method of search, all 202 potential participants in the pool were contacted to ask if they would be interested in participating in the study. Once participants agreed to participate in the study, they were sent a consent form, which was signed, and an email was sent to schedule a date and time that worked for the participants. Figure 4.1 displays the total participant pool ($N = 202$) that were contacted multiple times and the reasons to either become a participant or not.

Figure 4.1
Participant Pool Response Rate by Type

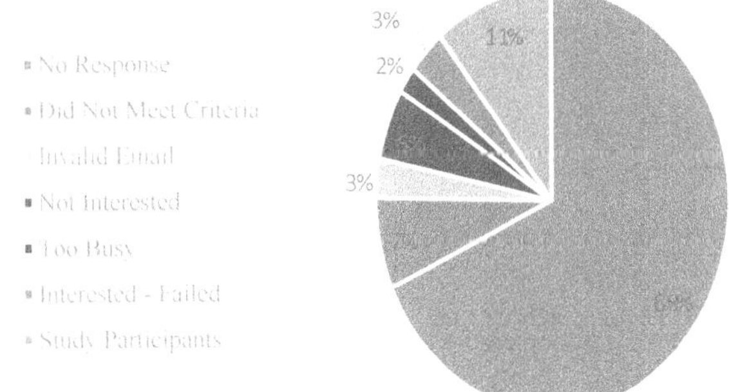

Note. The data of contacts were maintained by the researcher in an Excel spreadsheet that used tabs to separate the inquiries by state. As responses, or nonresponses, came in, each contact was color-coded to identify the types of responses.

As depicted in Figure 4.1, 68% of the potential participants did not respond to outreach that included email, LinkedIn, and phone calls. Additionally, 7% did not meet the criteria of either not having been in business within the date parameters or having more than 5 employees. Of the respondents, 5% did respond but had stated they were not interested and another 2% responded by stating they were too busy to participate. There were 3% of potential participants that responded with interest and after sending the consent form, there was no further response, even though several attempts were made to reconnect. A total of 3% of the email outreach resulted in bounced back emails that were invalid. Finally, out of the 202 outreach emails, LinkedIn, and phone calls, a total of 11% participated in the study. In summary, there were six main sources of how the final 22 participants were found, as exhibited in Figure 4.2.

Figure 4.2

Source of Participants

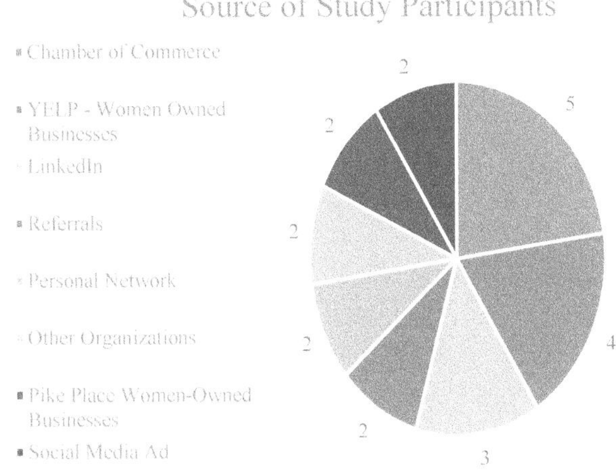

Note. The snowball sampling technique did not result in any referrals. A social media ad or post was placed on LinkedIn and Facebook to identify potential participants. Additionally, there was a column included in the Excel spreadsheet that was maintained by the researcher titled source, which indicated how the participants were contacted.

The 22 participants were a diverse representation of the Pacific Northwest states, employee sizes, and types of businesses. Table 4.1 represents the geographic location (i.e., state and number of counties) of the participants. The study participants' geographical location represents 13 counties in the Pacific Northwest. Table 4.2 displays the types of businesses by the number of employees, and Table 4.3 represents the industries the participants covered according to North American Industry Classification

System (NAICS) codes. There are a total of 20 NAICS codes classified under the U. S. Census Bureau (2024) and the participants in the study included 11 NAICS sectors. This means that the representation of participants represented more than 50% of the NAICS sectors.

Table 4.1

Participants' Geographic Location

State	# of participants	Counties represented
Idaho	2	2
Montana	2	1
Oregon	6	6
Washington	12	4
Total	22	13

Note. Upon outreach to 202 participants, there were a total of 22 participants, representing 13 counties across the Pacific Northwest, as defined by the Pacific Northwest Electric Power Planning and Conservation Act of 1980, and all businesses have been in operation for at least 5 to10 years, with the exception of two participants that have been in business for 20-plus years.

Table 4.2

Participants by Employee Size

Size	# of participants
0 employees	16
1 employee	3
2.5 employees	1
4 employees	2

Total   22

Note. Of the 22 participants in the study, a majority (*n* = 16) were

solopreneurs, meaning they had no other employee other than themselves.

Table 4.3

Industries Covered by NAICS Sector Classification Codes

NAICS sector code represented	NAICS sector description	Number of participants
11	Agriculture, forestry, fishing, and hunting	1
23	Construction	1
31–33	Manufacturing	2
44–45	Retail trade	6
53	Real estate and rental and leasing	1
54	Professional, scientific, and technical services	9
56	Admin. support\waste mgmt.\remediation services	1
62	Health care and social assistance	1
71	Arts, entertainment, and recreation	2
72	Accommodation and food services	2
81	Other services (except public administration)	1

Note. Using data from the U. S. Census Bureau (2024), all participant

businesses were identified by the NAICS code. The number of participants

represented under the NAICS code exceeds the number of participants

because some of the businesses are identified under multiple NAICS codes.

Data Analysis Procedure

Through the combination of researcher notes and the transcribed

interviews, the data analysis followed the hierarchical approach used in

qualitative research, which is preparing the raw data to be analyzed, followed by transcribing, reading, coding, and theming (Creswell & Creswell, 2018).

The final part of the hierarchical approach is interpreting or discussing the

meaning of the data, which is in Chapter 5. The steps outlined by Creswell

and Creswell (2018) that were used include (a) organizing and preparing the

data, (b) reading and looking at all the data, (c) coding the data, (d)

developing categories, (e) developing descriptions, (f) developing themes,

and finally, (g) interpreting the meaning of the data. The transcripts were read

and coded several times, using different strategies. The first strategy was

coding the data according to the research questions. The second strategy was

coding the data blindly, without any preconceived categories.

The process of interviewee transcript review was also used to ensure

credibility and validity, which is sharing the raw data of the interviews with

participants and can also increase participants' confidence and anonymity

(Rowlands, 2021), which did not result in any modifications to the original

transcripts. Each participant was supplied with a copy of the transcript and

provided an opportunity to review the data and to confirm the interview

represented their beliefs. Because the theoretical foundation for this study

took on a feminist view, it has been found that feminist researchers find it

valuable to complete interviewee transcript review in the research process as

it can lead to a meaningful exercise that includes participants' empowerment

(Chase, 2017; Rowlands, 2021; Varpio et al., 2017). None of the participants

made any changes to the interview transcripts; rather, all agreed the

information represented their words and beliefs.

In addition to human coding, NVivo V14 a computer-aided qualitative data analysis software (CAQDAS) software was used. NVivo V14 is the most used software tool used in qualitative and mixed-methods research (Ose, 2016). NVivo is privately licensed and not cloud-based for individual users (Lumivero.com, n.d.), which added another layer of confidentiality and rigor to the study (Maher et al., 2018). NVivo was not used to interpret any of the data; rather, it was used to organize the data. The researcher took the handmade codes and created them in NVivo and then moved blocks of texts to the categories that were created for ease of analyzing.

Presentation of Findings

The data for the presentation of findings came directly from the participant's answers to the semi-structured interview questions (see Appendix A), which emerged into the six themes. Table 4.4 is a summary of the categories that were used to arrive at the themes.

Table 4.4

Themes and Categories

Theme	Categories
Self-Sufficiency	Most important financial skill, knowing your numbers, financial position, savings, taxes, importance of monitoring finances, strategies
Support Systems	Holding back from acquiring new financial skills, acquisition of skills, tools used, accounting
Insignificant Skills/ Strategies	Least important financial skill, looking backwards, unpredictability, forecasting, competition, challenges
SARS-CoV-2 Impact	Challenges, impact of COVID-19, emotions

| Subject of Finance | Awareness of gender disparity, feelings, emotions, gender impact, least important financial skill, language |
| Sentiment of Passion | Love, inspiration, emotions |

Note. There were 25 categories that were used to arrive at the themes.

Table 4.5 is a display of the themes that emerged, along with a longer description of the meaning of the themes.

Table 4.5

Emerging Themes with Theme Description

Theme title	Theme description
Self-Sufficiency	Knowing your numbers is important to women microentrepreneurs to remain self-sufficient.
Support Systems	Women microentrepreneurs rely on a variety of tools and techniques to make financial decisions.
Insignificant Skills/Strategies	Traditional skills not used by microentrepreneurs: forecasting and competition.
SARS-CoV-2 Impact	COVID-19 impacted women microentrepreneurs both negatively and positively.
Subject of Finance	The topic of finance is intimidating and women microentrepreneurs find little value in increasing financial skills.
Sentiment of Passion	High levels of passion drive women microentrepreneurs to self-sufficiency.

Note. Descriptions of the themes have been supplied to assist with placing them into context.

The next section includes each theme in more detail, including direct quotes from participants. Each participant is represented in at least one theme, representing all 22 participants.

Theme 1: Self-Sufficiency

Knowing, understanding, and monitoring the financial numbers of the business has been found to be instrumental for 20 out of 22 participants who have indicated that the action of knowing their numbers leads them to self-sufficiency. This is supported by book that indicates paying attention to the business results in positive performances, such as increased revenues, profits, sales, customers, and product lines (Waziri & Nnko, 2023).

Being self-sufficient means the business is profitable, steady, and all are making enough money to pay their bills and remain in business. Being able to support their lifestyle by being self-sufficient was a common theme throughout the study and regardless of what that may mean to others, participants have indicated that it is not up to others to label their business in terms of good, very good, stable, growing, or profitable. Rather, PE indicated, "From a financial point of view, some might consider that it's not doing so great, but for me, it's meeting my needs. I feel like it's doing fantastic, like way better than I ever could have expected." PB elaborated on the

unimportance of what others use to describe their business by adding:
> It's successful. And how I define that is by am I making enough to hey? To support my life, to support myself and my husband? You know we can. I pay the mortgage. Can I pay my bills? I can fund my life through the work that I do.

Monitoring their finances has led participants to make informed decisions about the business. When asked if it was important to monitor their finances, PQ responded, "[It's] huge, huge, huge, huge. If you don't pay attention to the business side. you will not be in business for long." This sentiment was

reiterated by PO who stated, "It's absolutely necessary to make sure that your

costs are covering your expenses . . . to not have an eye on your numbers can

really kick you in the teeth." PB explained why it is important to know your

numbers and uses it as a means of analyzing purchases. PB stated:

> [I] would say, it's very, very important for the success of your
> business. Well, it has allowed me to truly understand what my income
> is. It's allowed me to review expenses and in a way that you know, I
> can kind of just analyze and say, Is this worth it?

Although all participants indicated that monitoring the finances is important,
2 out of the

22 participants did not support the description of their business being self-

sufficient; rather, they turned to a secondary source of income to support their

business. PI described her financial position as very weak, and PR described

her position as unstable.

In summary, 20 out of 22 participants have described the financial

performance of their business as self-sufficient, whether it was because they

had enough to pay the bills or meet their needs, which was important to them.

The two participants that did not define themselves as self-sufficient relied on

supplemental income to keep the business running. The next section

discusses how monitoring the finances of their business has enabled

participants to employ pricing strategies.

Pricing

Knowing and monitoring the finances of their business have also

enabled several participants to be able analyze their costs, expenses, and worth, and as a result, raise prices. A total of 64% (14 out of 22) of the

participants indicated that keeping an eye on business numbers has enabled

them to evaluate their business and make changes to their pricing structure.

PD indicated that one of the most important financial skills a businessperson

should have is knowing how to price their products or services and stated,

"Number one is pricing either services or products where you've got to take

into account your labor and material and markup cause I want to charge what

I'm worth." PI also indicated that pricing in what costs to produce a product

or service is dependent on including the value of their own time:

> People would tell me . . . just call around and see what everyone's
> charging. I was like. This is ridiculous. I don't. It doesn't matter what
> other people are charging. It matters what it costs me to take care of
> this horse.

Including their own labor in pricing structure was also supported by PL, who
stated:

> Figuring out your price points is very important to make sure that you
> know, while you want it to be within an industry standard to make sure
> that you're not under selling it. Including your labor, which is really
> hard to do at first.

In summary, understanding their numbers, such as costs, expenses, and sales

are particularly important to women microentrepreneurs. The description of

their financial position varied but was primarily considered self-sufficient. In

general, the participants have concluded that personally paying attention to

their numbers has proven to benefit them in running their business. Some

participants also added that directly examining their numbers and knowing

them very well has enabled them to price their products and services to

include the value they bring to the business.

Theme 2: Support Systems

The results of the interviews have indicated that women

microentrepreneurs rely on a variety of tools and techniques to make

financial decisions. As indicated in Chapter 2, a report by the U.S. Congress

in 2021 considers the knowledge of the "tools that equip people to make

individual financial decisions and take action to attain their goals" (Cooper,

2021, p. 3) as a part of financial literacy. The findings from this study

indicated that this is common with the women microentrepreneurs that were

interviewed. The tools and techniques used by the participants come in the

form of support and tools, fintech, and savings, which are explained in more

detail next.

Support and Tools

There are a variety of tools the participants turned to for financial

information. More than 50% (13 out of 22) have looked to family and friends

specifically, and all participants used resources outside of family and friends

including the internet, financial professionals, consultants, books, other

business owners, fintech, and nonprofit entities. Table 4.6 is a summary of

where the participants gain financial knowledge to make decisions.

Table 4.6

Sources of Financial Knowledge to Make Financial Decisions

# of participants	Acquisition of financial knowledge
15	Internet and online resources
8	Other business owners

5	Nonprofit organization resources
18	Outsource bookkeeping, accounting and Certified Public Accountant (CPA) services
19	Fintech tools

Note. Internet resources mentioned included Google, Facebook groups, networking groups, and online videos. Additionally, the number of participants column exceeded the number of participants that were interviewed because some of the participants used more than one resource.

PH elaborated on the support she received from family and friends, noting:

> I would say that he [ex-boyfriend] probably was a big, instrumental person in my life who probably put me on that path of making sure savings was always a thing for me. Okay, so that was definitely my dad. But my ex-boyfriend probably helped.

Similarly, PM used family support and internet resources and stated, "So I go quickly to him [husband]. Otherwise, I would do some online. It's just online, just Googling." PL also looked to Google to find quick answers but also has turned to nonprofit resources and stated, "I did take some courses through Seattle the Greater Seattle SCORE regarding the financial things so I could actually understand what was going on a little bit more." PQ spoke about how she worked with other business owners to aid in her financial knowledge:

> A friend who had been in business longer like 20 [years], like quite a bit longer, you know. A trusted advisor, I would say, like somebody who had already gone through it. And similar business.

Eighteen out of 22 participants outsourced financial tasks to a finance professional. This did not necessarily mean they use someone regularly, although some did. Many used the resources for filing their end-of-year taxes.

Eight out of the 18 participants indicated that outsourcing financial tasks to others is beneficial to them because it has enabled them to focus on their strengths and leave the financial part to an expert. PN stated, "I mean, I don't think you really need to know how to do the accounting, because you can really hire people to do that." This sentiment was mimicked by seven other participants. PJ has an educational background in business and considered it the most important skill for business owners to have; however, she still turned to external professional support.

Of the four participants who did not use an external financial professional for bookkeeping, accounting, or tax services, one of the participants ran a professional bookkeeping service, another did her own bookkeeping and taxes, and two made no mention of using an external professional for bookkeeping or taxes.

Outsourcing financial tasks is a means to acquiring knowledge and the participants used a variety of sources such as family and friends, other business owners, and networking, which has been supported in research as being important for mentorship and guidance (I. Liu, 2023).

Fintech

Results from this study concluded that 19 out of 22 participants used some form of financial technical tools or fintech to monitor their finances. The use of fintech has been found to have positive impacts to entrepreneurs such as improved efficiency, growth, financial performance, and flexibility (Sharma et al., 2023). The participant's most popular use of fintech is

Quickbooks (10 participants), followed by Excel (seven participants), and then Square (5 participants). Of the three participants who did not use any form of fintech, they used what they called the *old school* way of recording everything, which is writing it down. PI indicated:

> It is literally putting down old school on a, you know, ledger. The category, I mean. That's how I do it. I have this big, long thing. I have like 20 things on the top, and then I have them coming down here and then just writing every single thing, I think that it also reminds me of the hard work. It's not just click, click, click, it makes it real.

PM reiterated the old school technique by stating, "I do everything manually. I don't have any, you know, solid software or anything. I do everything manually. I write down everything. So, a very old school."

The use of fintech is supported by book in Chapter 2, in that it provides efficiency in business through automated tasks such as bill paying and most of the participants use some form of Fintech to streamline business operations.

Savings

Another technique used by participants is savings. One of the core components, according to the Organization for Economic Cooperation and Development (2022) and the *Big Five* financial literacy assessment (Global Financial Literary Excellence Center,

n.d.) that is used worldwide is saving, and many of the participants follow this basic tenet of financial literacy. Sixteen out of the 22 participants have a savings account, and the reason for having savings varies between two categories: (a) saving for unexpected expenses and (b) saving specifically for taxes. Unexpected incidents can occur at any time, and PG explained why she saves:

> So, you need to be making enough so that you have your expense[s] covered, but also that little cushion, because, like we had an ice storm in January, and it shut us all down for a week. I knew the business is gonna be okay because I had a cushion.

PH shared how her mentality for savings was something ingrained in her at an early age, which she carries through to today. PH shared her story of how she learned to save from her father:

> What I remember was two things, he said. If you show me how much is in your savings account, and I remember this. I don't remember the timing. I will match your savings account. And I do remember that I always remember that. And funny that I just found a card that had the clip of the check that he gave me. Isn't that funny? And so, it was probably like $1,500 I saved, and so he matched it.

Fourteen participants indicated they have a savings account for taxes, and 50% of participants used a process of taking a percentage of each sale to put aside for taxes. PB stated, "I put aside one third of every invoice that I have for taxes."

In summary, the participants have partaken in a variety of tools and techniques to keep their businesses running. The tools used to acquire financial information come from various resources including family, friends, fintech, the internet, fellow business owners, and financial experts. Another technique that was employed by the participants was having savings for either the big and unexpected things or saving for taxes.

Theme 3: Insignificant Skills and Strategies

All the participants in the study have indicated there is a specific skill and strategy that have been traditionally used in business they have found to be insignificant in their business, which were long-term financial forecasting and competing with others. Rather than formal financial forecasting, as described by Boyles (2022), 19 out of 22 participants indicated their reason for not forecasting long-term was mostly because of the unpredictability, dealing with the ebbs and flows of the business, and juggling to meet their monthly needs. Of the 19 participants who did not forecast long-term, 5 indicated that forecasting was the least important financial skill needed for their business. Competition was found to be of no value to 20 out of 22 participants; rather, it was more important to focus on their own business.

Financial Forecasting

Financial forecasting is defined as the process of looking at historical data to project what may happen in the future (Boyles, 2022), and four common methodologies are used: (a) straight-line, (b) moving average, (c) simple linear regression, and (d) multiple linear regression. There was one participant who historically did not forecast; however, she has recently adopted formal long-term forecasting because her business model had changed. Additionally, PH forecasted early in her career but no longer finds it valuable because she has been in business for over 30 years, is well-established, and has created a name for her business.

One of the reasons for not forecasting was due to the unpredictability of business, as indicated by PS who stated that forecasting is "all a crap shoot." PM supported unpredictability, and she stated:

> I can get that when you feel like things are going really great. It's like over your shoulder. And then next week, I'm like, I have no sessions [and] become like, what's going on it's so unpredictable. Can I do anything to project that? I cannot predict because I just cannot.

Although the participants do not do any long-term financial forecasting due to unpredictability, two have indicated that if they have a big project on a contractual basis, they can predict revenue based on the duration of the contract. PT said, "We're in a 2year project and they pay me monthly. So that's kind of a new way I can forecast."

Another form of forecasting is by using variability analysis, looking backwards at data points to arrive at averages to predict future earnings (Scott, 2020). A total of 11 out of 22 participants used variability forecasting. PL shared:

> I often will look at least 4 to 6 months also in reverse so I can kind of come up with some projections. I can look at the past year to see what I hope to do. A lot of the projections really comes from looking backwards.

PK supported the notion of looking backwards by stating, "Well, probably I'm always looking at it backwards, I don't know that I do a lot of forecasting. I['m] kind of a 'hope for the best type' of person."

Five participants indicated there were external forces beyond their control as one of the reasons they do not forecast such as the weather, economy, and inflation. PI shared:

It's not a type of business where you can say well, we have this much to
budget for. It doesn't work that way, because I'm also depending on
what's gonna happen with the weather. How many of the water rights that
are allotted to the hay farmers that year?

In summary, formal financial forecasting is not something that the

participants of the study partake in. Rather, they find business to be so

unpredictable to forecast because of forces beyond their control (e.g.,

weather, the economy). If there is any formal financial forecasting, it is based

on established contracts the participants have with customers but not on day-

to-day customers. The next section discusses another formal strategy that was

not used by the participants, which was engaging in competitive wars.

Ignoring the Competition

According to the Small Business Administration (SBA),

competitiveness is a way for small businesses to gain an advantage over

others in the same industry (SBA, 2024), and book has indicated that

financial literacy can contribute toward business growth, success, and a

competitive advantage (Anshika, 2022; Baporikar & Akino, 2020).

However, 20 out of 22 participants in this study indicated that paying

attention to the competition was a waste of time and rather than competing

with others. PG stated,

"There's so much ocean out there and so many boats that there's plenty for

all of us." Rather than working against the competition or practicing

competitiveness, they work and learn from others in their industry. PD stated,

"I look for other business owners that have been successful and learn from

them." PG expanded on her thoughts on competing with others and stated:

> So, networking. again, like talking with other small business owners,
> specifically food businesses. The other bakery that's in town who she
> was my competitor, but now she's not. She and I exchange information
> all the time and ask each other questions about things and that's super
> helpful.

Other sentiments on competing were voiced by PH who said, "Don't need to

pay attention to maybe worrying about what other people are doing. Create

your own path." PJ supported that by saying:

> How to be successful is really this kind of like dog eat dog mentality
> where it's like you are successful over other people. Spending a lot of
> time worrying about that seems like a waste of time to me. If I spend a
> lot of time worried about going online and getting all of the clients and
> beating my colleagues at winning the clients I could very easily spend
> way too much time on that, and not giving my clients that I have the
> care that they need, and that ultimately is gonna lose me business.

Not paying attention to what others are doing has been found to be beneficial

to most participants and PK indicated that although she does not look

externally to compete, she competes with herself. This was also indicated by

PQ who shared that she did not worry about the competition because despite

competition existing, the value of what she brings to the table is her true goal.

In summary, the women microentrepreneurs that were interviewed did

not use the traditional skill of forecasting and strategy of competing with

others valuable to them. Rather, the common way to project how well a given

month would result might be to practice variability, the process of looking

backward at previous years or months. Due to the unpredictability of the

business, many do not practice looking to the future because they found it to

be a waste of time. If a participant had a long-term contract with another

business entity, they would forecast that revenue for the duration of the contract, but everything else was so unpredictable. Finally, there were some the participants that did not forecast because of external forces that were beyond their control (e.g., economy, inflation, weather), which have a huge influence on their business. Finally, most of the participants did not feel a need to compete with others in the same industry. Rather, they compete with themselves, use other business owners' advice, and pay attention to what they are doing, not what others are doing.

Theme 4: SARS-CoV-2 Impact

The COVID-19 pandemic impacted the women entrepreneurs in this study negatively and positively. All participants indicated negative impacts during the pandemic, due to mandatory shutdowns and going without an income for the duration. The pandemic brought about new challenges for all of humanity, including economic, social, environmental, educational, and health setbacks (Miyah et al., 2022) and the participants in this study were not immune to these challenges. However, contrary to the negative impacts of the pandemic, 19 out of 22 participants realized positive impacts.

Some of the negative impacts from the COVID-19 pandemic indicated by the participants included it being a challenging and stressful time, and some felt it was going to be the end of their business. PA stated, "My initial reaction was to hide in the corner and suck my thumb. I thought it was done. I'm like, oh, well, I'm screwed." PO supported this by saying, "I was open the whole entire time because we're considered a restaurant and had I not been able to stay open. Yeah, we wouldn't have survived." There were also other emotional mentions during the COVID-19 pandemic. PH stated it caused "more stress," PJ indicated it was a "significant struggle," PE mentioned "it was a challenging time," and PM indicated "it was very hard."

Although all experienced negative impacts due to the COVID-19 pandemic, 19 out of 22 participants indicated the pandemic also had a positive impact on their business, which aligned with Manolova et al.'s (2020) findings. The following participants explained how they pivoted their businesses to stay in business during the pandemic. PE stated, "During those 4 months, you worked a lot on repairs [instead of core craft] and even met with clients outside, wearing masks and gloves to keep the business running." PL used a variety of ways to pivot her business to remain relevant in the market. PL stated:

> I started making I crochet as well. So, I crocheted some human hats, and then during the pandemic, I developed some dog hats, so I've got some of those as well. You know, little bit between 2019 and 2020, because of the pandemic but still some growth, which is great like, I said, the good news is, I was able to keep going.

With only having a brick-and-mortar presence, PP realized she had to do something to remain open and created an entirely new product. PP stated:

> Well, many people were caught completely off guard, but a lot of us were not. You know. We were relying 100% on in-person sales. I didn't have a web presence. I didn't have an Etsy store. The pandemic kind of was a positive thing for me in the end. That was the best thing that ever happened to me, because it forced me to do things that I probably wouldn't have done.

Other positive impacts experienced by some of the participants were an increase in revenue from either being considered an essential business, transitioning to online, or because the industry they were in was advantageous to them. PA shared:

> This is where it was advantageous to be in corporate and commercial photography. The first thing that helped was at the time I had a contract with zoom care. I've had a contract with them which it didn't take long for them to get on the horn with me and say, that actually kind of makes you an essential worker because I had a written contract and they desperately needed photography. In 2020 my revenue doubled over my '21 revenue.

Aside from the positive monetary impacts of COVID-19, some of the realized benefits were not monetary; rather, the benefits included participants having the time to take a mental health break, care for family members, and be a support mechanism for their communities. PQ stated the mandatory shut-down led her to take a break and stated, "I was so burned out at that time when they said things are shut down for 2 weeks. I was like, oh my God, this is awesome! I could mentally take a break." PI added that her experience during COVID-19 was a blessing and stated:

> COVID, it was a great outlet for the kids. So, everyone was here all day and you know that's what God gave us this place for and that's what I wanted. I wanted to be full of kids and happiness and good families, and no money can replace that.

These are some of the examples expressed by the participants about the pandemic, with many finding positive ways to manage the challenging time.

In summary, the world was impacted by the COVID-19 pandemic, whether one was a business owner or not. There were mandatory shutdowns and lock downs throughout the world, and it was a new reality that had never been witnessed before. However, the resiliency of the women microentrepreneurs in this study supported other evidence of being able to pivot their business into something else, working extra hard to remain

relevant, realizing financial growth because of the industry they were in, and

stepping up as concerned citizens for others to act as a means of support

during the time of the pandemic.

Theme 5: Subject of Finance

Although many of the participants indicated that looking at their

numbers is vital for self-sustainability, the subject of finance has been found

to be intimidating and the women microentrepreneurs in this study found

little value in increasing their financial literacy skills due to lack of time,

costs of courses, and determining whether the course will add any value to

their business. Time has been documented as being a major constraint for

women microentrepreneurs, because they typically operate as a sole

proprietor, having to juggle a multitude of tasks (Gross, 2022). Participants

also perceived that acquiring additional or new financial skills was not

pursued because the topic of finance was intimidating. Table 4.7 summarizes

the frequency of participants mentioning the categories of time, money, or

value as a reason for not acquiring new financial skills.

Table 4.7

Lack of Time, Money, and Value

# of participants	Reasons for not acquiring additional financial skills
17	Time to learn additional financial skills was a problem to furthering their education.
8	Money to learn additional financial skills was the problem in furthering their education.
7	There was no perceived value of a course.

were interviewed because several participants mentioned more than one

reason for not acquiring additional financial literacy skills.

PJ indicated all three categories stand in the way of her acquiring

additional financial skills by stating, "Time and finance just not feeling that

the benefit is worth the expenditure of that." PK stated, "I'm already working

23 hours out of the day. Well, I'm sleeping, you know, for 4 hours. Then I'm

working. So where do you want me to fit this in to learn about these financial

skills?" PM indicated that in addition to running a business, other

responsibilities in life must be accounted for by stating, "I have two kids and

balancing it out as well. I have only so much time in a month."

As previously mentioned, 7 out of 22 participants indicated the value

they would get out of the course is what is impacting their decision to further

their education in financial literacy. PN stated:

> If I was interested, I would go for it. And people are usually really
> happy to help you out. With that, my experience with a lot of those
> things have been that it's someone selling something that rarely has
> value.

The value a course may bring was indicated by PC who stated, "non-profits

that offer all this help it doesn't necessarily apply to me."

In addition to the categories of time, money, and value, more than half

of the participants (14 out of 22) stated their feelings about the topic of

finance caused anxiety, shame, intimidation, and embarrassment. PT mentioned that finance is intimidating. PM added, "I think I'm just too intimidated with these things. And I feel like I would rather do something more creative." The feelings of intimidation and shame continued with comments from the participants, including PP who stated:

> I think a lot of us don't take those kinds of business classes because you're going to sit in front of somebody who's going to talk about stuff, and you're just like I don't want to raise my hand every time and look like an idiot.

PQ cathartically spoke about her feelings about finance and stated:

> In the beginning I had a lot of shame around money. I wasn't raised in money. My parents were both terrible with money. I couldn't ask them, and I always was just so scared I was doing it wrong because I had no educational background in it. You could work on getting a new lens or something, right? Or you can take a financial literacy course. It's hard. It's like, my brain doesn't get it, you know. So, I got that shame in the beginning.

As indicated by many scholars, there is a gender gap in financial literacy among men and women (Goyal & Kumar, 2021; Lusardi & Mitchell, 2007; Milken Institute, 2021), and the topic of finance was also viewed from a gender perspective. Participants were asked if they were aware of a gender disparity in financial literacy between men and women and if so, did they think it had an impact on their business. Table 4.8 summarizes the level of awareness of the participants.

Table 4.8

Participant Awareness Levels of Gender Disparity in Financial Literacy

Level	# of participants
Aware	15

| Not surprised | 4 |
| Unaware | 3 |

Note. Table 4.8 represents the level of awareness of the participants regarding the gendered awareness of financial literacy between men and women.

Taking the participants that were aware of the gender disparity and combining it with those that are not surprised brought the general awareness to 19 out of 22 participants. Table 4.9 summarizes the perceptions of the participant's responses to gender having an impact on their business due to the financial literacy gender disparity.

Table 4.9

Impact of Financial Literacy Gender Disparity on Business

# of participants	Impact on business
13	Negative impact on business operations.
7	No impact on business operations.
2	No indication on the impact of the gender disparity on business operations.

Note. Of the two participants who did not make an indication of the impact of the financial literacy gender disparity on business operations, one indicated she was aware of the gender disparity and the other participant indicated that she was not surprised.

The participants who were aware or not surprised of the gender disparity in financial literacy and had an impact on their business noted the reasons for this impact were the societal beliefs of women being more

nurturing, emotional, and empathetic (Ahl & Marlow, 2021). PN stated:

> Technically, I'm a license general contractor. I did the license general
> contractor, because especially a woman working in the trades, I really
> felt like I needed that layer of legitimacy. But I just felt like, like I said,
> like a woman in the industry. I just really needed to show that I was
> serious about my business and that this wasn't something you know
> that I was gonna be wishy washy about.

Regarding gender gaps, some of the participants mentioned it may have

something to do with confidence or men's and women's brains being wired

differently. For example, PJ indicated that she felt the perceptions of women

business owners were, "We don't have a head for business, or management or

things like that. So it's probably better to, you know, work for someone else,

or whatever." The participants in the study expressed they felt women had

softer emotions compared to men, which was perceived as having a negative

impact on their business. PV indicated that, "If there wasn't such a disparity,

[her] business would be doing better." The notion of earning more if they

were a man was not just a perception of PA. Rather, she was aware that she

has allowed her softer emotions to impact her earning potential. As indicated

by PA:

> My gender impact[s] my income potential. And if it comes down to
> one thing in particular, I've experienced and seen something. I have
> definitely seen that a lot of people know how to work a woman
> sometimes and play the emotional card to get discounts [and] that does
> work against me because I do have a soft heart, and I have definitely
> been known to give in, or freebie. I know I'm asked to either over
> deliver or under charge on disproportionately a higher level than most
> men in this field.

PB supported the ability to charge more if she were a man by stating, "I would be charging more if I was a man. I'm sad to say that but that is true."

Those that were aware or unaware of the financial literacy gender disparity but who did not feel impacted predominately stated it was because of the industry they were in. As indicated by PD, she was aware of the gender disparity; however, she did not think it had negatively impacted her business. PD stated:

> I actually think it's favorable to my business because most of my clients not all, but most of them are women. And I think they all feel like there's a lot of shame around money, and oftentimes, some of the men in financial services it just feels like there's judgment there and a little bit of talking down or using jargon that your average lay person, man or woman, doesn't know

PH supported this by stating, "I would say yes. Well, funny! I don't think it is true in my business, but I think that women in my industry do better."

In summary, when it came to attaining additional financial literacy skills through formal training, the participants were concerned with the time, cost, and the lack of value it might bring to their business. Another factor of not participating in formal financial training was attributed to the awareness of the gender disparity in financial literacy, with more than half of the participants indicating it had an impact on their business. The next section discusses how the use of financial nomenclature used in formal training courses and academia act as a deterrent to acquiring additional financial skills.

Use of Language

Time, money, and the value of pursuing additional financial skills stand in the way of many of the participants to not partake in additional financial literacy courses. In addition to time, money, and value, many of the participants felt intimidated by the topic of finance. However, through analyzing the interview data, many of the participants used many of the skills that were defined in the financial world as something different than described by the participants. There are three finance areas where different words or language were used: (a) return on investment, (b) diversification, and (c) reconciliation.

More than 50% of the respondents used other language instead of the finance nomenclature, which is commonly used to measure financial literacy worldwide (Lusardi, 2019; Organisation for Economic Co-operation and Development (OECD) 2023; Urban & Valdes, 2022). Furthermore, many of the respondents acknowledged that finance is a confusing language.

PP explained the various aspects of her business, which included a brick-andmortar shop and an online presence. Throughout the entire conversation, there was no mention of the financial term for what she was doing, which is diversifying to minimize risks. As PP explained, "I can only do the market because that's all you've got. So, I've been trying to expand and rely more on my website because I can resell things. So, my focus has been a little different." PK also explained how she uses three sources to sell her product without using the word diversification. PK said:

An interesting thing for me. I have a trailer that I take up and do pop ups with that. So, I go out in the community to different events. I started an online store right at the beginning of 2020, which was another blessing. Because if I hadn't had my online store up and running when COVID hit I would have been in a lot of trouble.

PG shared how she used a service for resourcing things and felt the cost was worth it because it enabled her to spend more time on the more important aspects of her business. She explained return on investment without using the financial nomenclature. PG said:

And one of the things that I utilize is a company [to] resource anything you need, even if he has to buy it online, he'll resource it. So most online stuff I do myself. He charges 8% off our bill for him to do that, and it's valuable to me, [rather than] spending all of my time, which is better spent in-house.

PU also spoke about the use of diversifying by stating, "I'm trying to figure out ways to teach art classes also, and that's kind of been getting me through the times when I don't have custom projects. So, I teach like small group art classes at the studio here." The language of finance was also mentioned as being something challenging. PA stated:

You can think of that is a commonly used term in finance that you would say, why don't they just call it this. Yeah, the term [s] used to make me cry. The acronyms can overwhelm If you're not programmed like that. Over time [I] have learned that it's certainly not my first language.

PM supported the language issue by stating, "Just because I don't know the terms that are taught in textbooks doesn't mean I don't know how to run a successful business." PO went on to discuss the language issue in finance when it came to filling out forms during the COVID-19 pandemic, and she stated:

And then you put language barriers into it, and then it was a complete
and total disaster, and I wouldn't have been able to fill out those forms
had it not been for Jamie, who is the bookkeeper and all of this
terminology. Yeah, it was a setup for failure.

In summary, the topic of finance to further educate microentrepreneurs is a

challenge because these small businesses do not have the time and if they did,

they were unsure of the value it would bring to their business. In addition to

the time and value, many of the participants indicated their perception of

finance is an intimidating topic, and the gender disparity does not help to ease

the intimidation. Rather, it exacerbates it, and many feel it has an impact on

their earning potential. Finally, when answering the semi-structured interview

questions, many participants indicated financial tasks they performed but did

not used financial nomenclature, rather they described the tasks in their own

way and have indicated that finance is a language unto itself.

Theme 6: Sentiment of Passion

The entrepreneurship characteristic of passion resonated in every

interview, which was a driving force for women entrepreneurs in this study to

remain self-sufficient. Although passion is not a financial skill, it has been

correlated to entrepreneurial performance and considered essential to

entrepreneurship as indicated in the book (Cardon et al., 2009; Hu et al.,

2022). PA explained:

I was exposed to it from my dad. Dad was a photographer most of my
young life, and so he went and bought me a camera for Christmas, and
it was like that was the beginning of the end. It took me very little time
to realize I was already having more fun.

PB supported this by stating, "What makes it feel so satisfying is that you know it's just me, and so that's what made me so passionate about it." Other sentiments of passion can be found in statements made by PE, who stated, "I found that I was really passionate about trade, really fascinated by it, very intrigued by it." PF expressed her passion by stating, "I loved the thought process that it helped me go through. When I was thinking about having employees, instead of being an employee, it brought a whole other level of interest in my own work."

PG expressed how doing what she does provides joy to others and indicated, "I really loved it, and I could be creative in a way that everybody enjoyed not just drawing on a piece of paper that only I enjoyed. It's the most rewarding." PK included that her passion for what she does is not only for herself, but it provides her with a connection to her customers. PK said:

> I like buying the clothes, going to market, bringing things back, getting excited, making that connection with my customer, being excited for them to be excited about something that's coming in. I like decorating my store and dressing the mannequins. That is like a creative outlet for me. I enjoy that. It's my happy place.

PM indicated that passion is the single thing that brought her into the world of entrepreneurship and stated, "I started this business purely out of passion, and I didn't know what passion actually meant when I even started it because I used to just shoot because I loved it so much." In summary, passion has been proven to be an essential asset in entrepreneurship and all the participants interviewed expressed some form of passion, whether it was their business being their *happy place*, finding it *rewarding*, and having enough passion to enter the world of entrepreneurship.

Summary

There were six themes that emerged from the analysis of the interviews as it relates to women microentrepreneurs and financial literacy. Theme 1 identified that knowing the ins and outs of their business finances was key to most of the participants having a financial position of self-sufficiency. In addition to describing their financial position as growing, profitable, successful, or good, examining their numbers and dissecting where every penny goes has enabled many of the participants to realize that their time and value is an important consideration when it comes to pricing their products and services.

Theme 2 emerged from the data analysis as learning about the tools and techniques that participants engaged in to acquire financial skills. Among the tools that were used, they varied from internal and external resources. Internal resources came from family and friends, and externally, a variety of sources are used. The participants turn to the internet, YouTube, Google, nonprofit organizations, Certified Public Accountants, bookkeepers, and other business owners to learn about financial techniques, and find answers to questions they may have when it comes to financial decisions. Another common tool used was fintech, which has helped businesses to keep track of their sales, expenses, customers, and continually check the health of their business.

In addition to the tools mentioned previously, there were two techniques the participants used to achieve self-sustainability. The first was having savings for the unexpected or to stay ahead of taxes so that it did not come as a shocking surprise or an unexpected event. As savings is a key tenet of financial literacy, this provided a window into how the participants were in tune with the importance of savings. The other technique the participants used was not competing with others in the same industry. Rather, they found that working together with others was a valuable resource for them to learn from.

Theme 3 was finding that long-term financial forecasting was not a focus for women microentrepreneurs. Being a microenterprise (i.e., 0 to 4 employees), many feel that small businesses are faced with such unpredictability that it was not worth their valuable time to forecast into the future, and it did nothing for their self-sustainability. The extent of ebbs and flows in small businesses were not necessarily seen in larger organizations and planning or forecasting was not a realistic endeavor.

The other form of forecasting typically comes from variability, which is looking backwards at previous months or years to determine what the current month or year should look like, financially. This provided the participants with a snapshot of what a month or a quarter could look like and was used as a marker to determine a goal for sales.

Theme 4 was the impact the COVID-19 pandemic had on these businesses, which resulted in negative and positive impacts. There was no disputing that the pandemic had negative impacts on everyone in any industry or location. There were so many unknowns during that time, and news from experts changed daily. Therefore, the negative emotions that were experienced by many were also experienced by the women microentrepreneurs who were interviewed. They did not know when things would open back up again, it caused additional work for sanitary purposes, and mandatory shutdowns impacted sales.

However, despite the negative impacts, many of the participants experienced positive impacts from the pandemic.

Some of the positive impacts aligned with previous book that found many women business owners pivoted their business during the COVID-19 pandemic (Manolova et al., 2020), and this was evident in the study. Many prospered during the pandemic based on their industry, and some prospered in a nonfinancial way by providing the participants with a mental health break from the craziness that was witnessed during that time.

Theme 5 was about finance being an intimidating subject to most participants, so much so that acquiring additional financial skills was not of value to them. Time, money, and value were the most common reasons for not acquiring additional financial literacy skills, followed by the intimidation of the topic of finance and an awareness of the gender disparity in financial literacy. Unbeknownst to many of the participants, they did, in fact, use many of the financial literacy skills that are defined in financial nomenclature;

however, there was a language difference, which lead to intimidation on the topic of finance.

Theme 6 was the characteristic of passion that led to self-sufficiency. All participants spoke of their business with passion, which was a driving force for them to continue to battle the ebbs and flows and ups and downs in their unpredictable environment.

To provide more context to the themes and words spoken by the participants,

Appendices B through G contain word clouds that are matched to each of the themes identified in Chapter 4. Chapter 5 discusses the findings and conclusions of the study.

Chapter 5 includes recommendations for future research and actions.

CHAPTER 5: CONCLUSIONS AND DISCUSSION

Women entrepreneurship in the U.S. has been on the rise with business formations as a percentage of all business formations have increased from 28% in 2019 to 49% in 2021 (Masterson, 2022). However, women in the U.S. have been considered less financially literate based on quantitative results, which have caused inequalities in entrepreneurship such as external access to funding, loan disapprovals, and survival rates. The researcher used a feminist lens to explore the meaning, knowledge, and use of financial literacy skills of women microentrepreneurs in the Pacific Northwest in the U.S. before, during, and post COVID-19. The data were aimed at answering three research questions to assist in identifying the perceptions of financial literacy and its impact on business, how financial skills are acquired, and the strategies and challenges experienced by microentrepreneurs. Interviews with 22 women microentrepreneurs were conducted to explore their views on financial literacy. There were six themes that emerged from the data analysis, which are displayed in Table 5.1 and were also included in Chapter 4.

Table 5.1

Emerging Themes

Theme	Theme title
Theme 1	Self-sufficiency
Theme 2	Support systems
Theme 3	Insignificant skills and strategies
Theme 4	SARS-CoV-2 impact
Theme 5	Subject of finance
Theme 6	Sentiment of passion

Each of the themes were explained in Chapter 4, and Chapter 5 analyzes the findings through a discussion of the findings including how the findings can be applied to the problem statement, research questions, how the findings can be applied to business, and recommendations for action and further research. This is followed by a concluding statement.

Discussion of Findings and Conclusions

The discussion of findings elaborates on the interview questions the study aimed to answer, which resulted from immersion in the data to establish codes, categories, and themes. The research questions (RQ) were:

RQ1: What are women entrepreneurs' perceptions of the impact on their business through the lens of their current financial literacy?

RQ2: How do women entrepreneurs acquire the financial skills used in their business?

RQ3: What are the financial approaches, strategies, and challenges, if any, faced by women entrepreneurs?

Figure 5.1 is a visual representation of how the research questions aligned with the themes that emerged from the data analysis, and Appendix A includes the research questions along with the semi-structured interview questions that were developed to assist in arriving at themes.

Figure 5.1

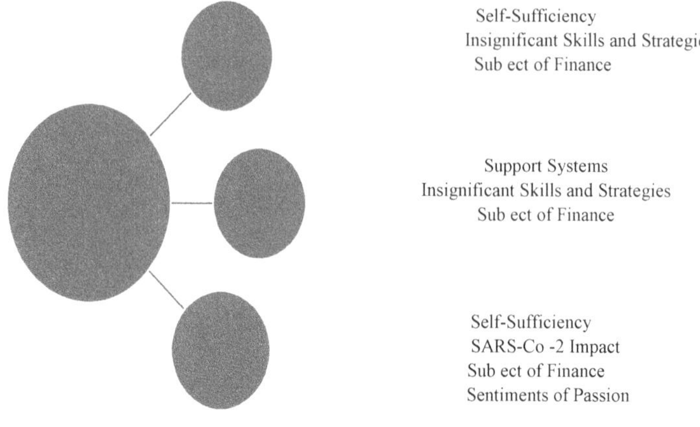

Research Question 1

Figure 5.2 is a visual representation of how the results of the study addressed the first research question about perceptions and impact along with the themes that aligned with the research question. RQ1 of the study was: "What are women entrepreneurs' perceptions of the impact on their business through the lens of their current financial literacy?"

Figure 5.2

Research Question 1 and Themes

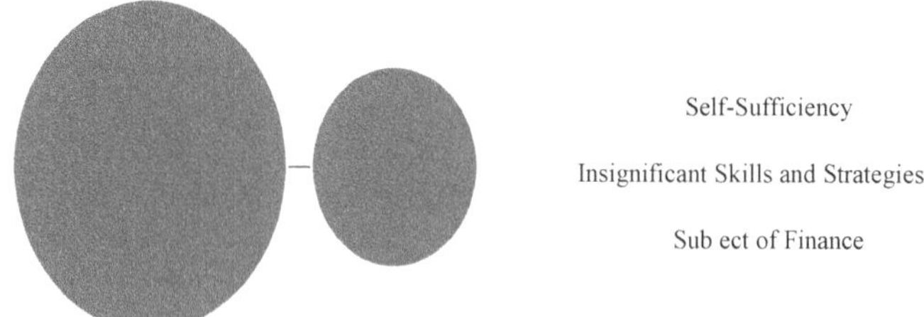

Three themes from the data analysis contributed toward answering RQ1 as detailed in Figure 5.2. This section is divided into three sections that include the importance of monitoring finances regularly, which contributes toward self-sufficiency, how financial forecasting long-term was insignificant to the participants, and the impact that the subject of finance has on acquiring additional financial skills.

Theme 1 was self-sufficiency. Knowing their numbers was important to women microentrepreneurs to remain self-sufficient and identified the perception of the impact of financial literacy on their business was critical. Twenty out of 22 microentrepreneurs interviewed considered themselves to be self-sufficient because they knew the importance of keeping track of the numbers of their business and they monitored their finances regularly, which can result in increased revenues, profits, sales, customers, and product lines (Waziri & Nnko, 2023). Self-sufficiency, as defined by the participants, means the business is profitable, steady, making enough money to pay the bills, and still being in business. The remaining two participants ran their businesses at a loss; however, they received funding from other jobs or their family. Therefore, when they file their year-end taxes, it results in a tax refund or rebate, which is then put back into the business, and these two participants indicated their businesses were weak and unstable.

Carefully monitoring their expenses has enabled 14 out of 22 participants to evaluate the pricing structures of their products and services to include their own labor, markups, and ensuring they are operating within industry standards. Although the participants are focusing on ensuring their pricing reflects their labor, book has indicated there has been an earnings gap in entrepreneurship. As indicated in book, a report by FreshBooks in conjunction with Research NOW (2018) reported the selfemployment wage gap stands at 28% with men earning, on average $77,540 versus women earning $56,184 (FreshBooks, 2018). This sentiment was mimicked by the participants in the study on their feelings about the gender disparity in entrepreneurship, with 13 out of 22 indicating that their gender had a negative impact on their business, financially.

Theme 3 identified another perception held by the participants, who did not find long-term financial forecasting to be beneficial to them because of the unpredictability of their business. Financial forecasting is defined as the process of looking at historical data to project what will happen in the future (Boyles, 2022), and rather than looking forward to forecasting for future possibilities, 19 out of 22 participants indicated the reason for not forecasting long-term was mostly because of the unpredictability, dealing with the ebbs and flows of the business, and juggling to meet their monthly needs. Of the 19 participants that did not conduct long-term forecasting, 5 indicated that forecasting was the least important financial skill needed for their business, and another 5 indicated they cannot conduct long-term forecasting because external forces such as the weather, inflation, and the economy have a hold on their ability to project forward. Not conducing long-term financial forecasting may be beneficial to the microentrepreneurs in this study, as financial forecasting has been linked to making poor decisions, because forecasting sets a reference point for the business owner, and when that reference point is not met, it leads to riskier decision making (Shrader et al., 2021). Therefore, rather than spending time on long-term financial forecasting, the participants were eliminating a form of risk.

Another form of forecasting is by using variability analysis or looking backwards at data points to arrive at averages to predict future earnings, as indicated in the book. There were 11 out of 22 participants that use variability forecasting. The three participants that did look forward financially do so because one participant just changed her business model into a cost-sharing operation and as a group, they project as far out as 2 years. The other two participants look forward financially because they have contracts that are long-term. However, they do not forecast forward on the normal day-to-day clients. The forecasting conducted by these three participants are not long-term or comprehensive for the entire business.

Theme 5 indicated that acquiring additional financial skills was avoided because the participants perceived the topic of finance as intimidating. Fourteen out of 22 participants stated that their feelings about the topic of finance caused anxiety, shame, intimidation, and embarrassment. Some of the 14 participants attributed these feelings to the focus of their business, which is more creative, and some felt shame around the topic of finance from an early age. Other descriptive words that were used by three participants around finance were "confusion," "stress," and "a black void."

An additional three participants felt the use of financial nomenclature was a

way for someone else to think that they were better or smarter than them.

There was one participant who did not know there was a term of "financial

literacy" and googled it prior to the interview, and another participant stated

that she has not thought about financial matters because she had been in

survival mode for so long but is planning to delve into finance more.

Interestingly, although there is fear, shame, and anxiety around

finance, more than 50% of the participants used other nomenclature instead

of the finance nomenclature often found in academia and research. As an

example, The Consumer Financial Protection Bureau (n.d.) publishes a

glossary of financial terms that are intended for educators to teach youth

financial literacy. Although the participants felt that finance is a confusing

language, many have partaken in the skills identified with financial

nomenclature such as "return on investment," "diversification," and

"reconciliation" but describe these financial terms in a different manner. As

indicated in book, diversification is one of the key elements in the financial

literacy assessments that are administered worldwide (Fisher & Ryan, 2021;

Milken Institute, 2021; World Bank,

n.d.). Because participants in the study did not use that specific term, it could

be a telltale sign of misunderstandings of functions that are performed but

referred to differently, which could be the cause of the gender gap in financial

literacy. As an example, one participant spoke about how she runs a brick-

and-mortar shop, has expanded to an online shop, and takes part in pop-up shows, which is an example of diversifying operations.

In summary, the participants' perception of the impact on their business through the lens of their current financial literacy is critical and their current financial literacy is attained through knowing their numbers well enough to make decisions to remain a tenable business. The participants in the study did this by monitoring their finances closely and regularly. Some have realized that pricing is a key metric to keep an eye on, which has enabled some to increase prices. There were others that realized savings is essential to tenability, whether it is for saving for any unexpected expenses and taxes. Another finding concluded that, a traditional skill used in business is forecasting, as indicated in the book review, which was not practiced by the microentrepreneurs in this study. This does not mean that they did not set up goals for themselves. Rather, they did not use long-term forecasting methods such as straight-line, moving average, simple linear regression, and multiple linear regression. The participants relied on looking backwards and setting goals. Finally, there was a perception of fear, shame, and anxiety around finance and money, which was another factor of why the participants did not seek out formal financial training.

Research Question 2

Figure 5.3 is a visual representation of how the results of the study addressed the second RQ about acquisition of financial skills with the themes that aligned with the RQ. RQ2 of the study was: "How do women

entrepreneurs acquire the financial skills used in their business?"

Figure 5.3

Research Question 2 and Themes

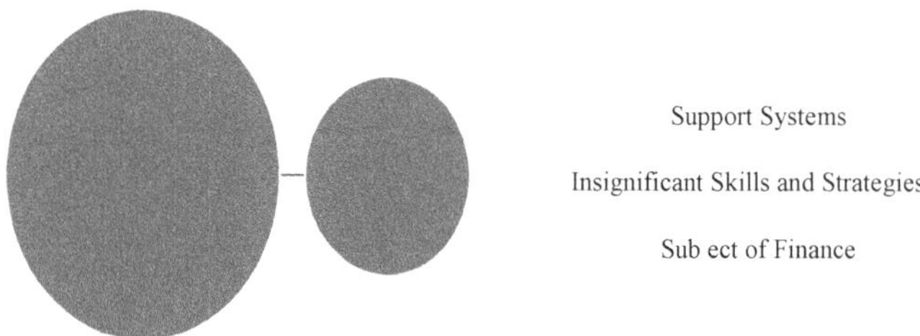

There were three themes from the data analysis that contributed toward

answering RQ2 as detailed in Figure 5.4. This section is divided into three

sections that include the constraints of acquiring new financial skills, tools

and techniques that were used to gain financial knowledge to make better

financial decisions, and how formal forward financial forecasting is

insignificant to the participants and were revealed through three themes.

Theme 5 identified that although few have taken formal courses to

further their financial skills, they did not pursue acquiring new financial skills due to the following constraints, as outlined in Table 5.2, and indicated in

Chapter 4.

Table 5.2

Lack of Time, Money, and Value

# of participants	Reasons for not acquiring additional financial skills
17	Time to learn additional financial skills was the problem to furthering their education.
8	Money to learn additional financial skills was the problem in furthering their education.
7	There was no perceived value of a course.

Note. This table is being repeated from Chapter 4 for ease of reference to the reader.

Several participants mentioned more than one category. In total, 21 out

of 22 participants indicated one or more of the categories of time, cost, and

value as a constraint to acquiring new financial skills. The one participant

that did not respond was because the question was skipped during the

interview in error. The time factor was consistent with Gross's (2022)

research that found women microentrepreneurs who primarily operated as a

sole proprietor managed various tasks, which limited their time to devote to

other areas in the business. Bank of America (2024) also concluded that 34%

of women business owners have caregiving responsibilities in addition to

running their business, versus 23% of men business owners. The participants

in this study also indicated the value of the courses that were offered was not

worth the limited amount of time they have because the information being taught does not relate to their business, and they felt the courses were geared more toward larger businesses. These feelings are supported in Chapter 2 with research conducted by Abdul Latif Jameel Poverty Action Lab (2023) and concluded that courses offered to microentrepreneurs had only modest impacts on key business outcomes.

Although formal channels were not the go-to for the participants in the study, another theme that emerged from the data analysis was Theme 2, which indicated that all participants used some form of support to gain financial knowledge to make informed decisions about their business. These forms of support may not necessarily add to a financial skill set; however, it did help them in finding solutions to their needs. Theme 2 indicated that women microentrepreneurs relied on a variety of tools and techniques for decision making. This was consistent with the book in Chapter 2, whereby Laguia et al. (2019) found that entrepreneurs use various sources for information to find ways to take advantage of opportunities and communicate the validity, strength, and value of their business. The variety of sources used for the acquisition of financial information included using fintech tools, the internet and online resources, family and friends, outsourcing to financial professionals, other business owners, and nonprofit organizations. Further discussion of the two most common sources for acquiring financial information, fintech and outsourcing, follows.

Fintech

Fintech are tools that use apps, software, or technology that enables businesses and consumers to digitally manage their finances to gain insights and conduct transactions (Trificana, 2023). Examples of fintech includes tools that help to streamline financial transactions for individuals and entrepreneurs including online banking, crowdfunding modeling, bill paying, and peer-to-peer lending (Sharma et al., 2023). Chapter 2 also indicated that entrepreneurs who incorporate some form of fintech into their businesses have positive impacts including improved efficiency, growth, and financial performance, flexibility for women microenterprises, and assist with overcoming financial stress (Sharma et al., 2023). This finding was supported by the results of this study. Nineteen out of 22 of the participants in the study use fintech tools, such as QuickBooks and Square, to monitor expenses, sales, and automate tax deductions on sales. These tools have enabled them to monitor their expenses, create invoices, and set aside money for taxes. Of the three participants that did not use any form of fintech, they used what they call the *old school* way of recording everything, which is writing it down without using fintech tools or AI.

Outsourcing

The second most common method for acquiring financial knowledge to make better decisions was through outsourcing to financial professionals. This can come in many forms such as networking with financial professionals, which has been found to be beneficial in entrepreneurship as it can aid in building relationships to acquire resources in the form of funding, business skills, and business services (Redd & Wu, 2020). Research also has indicated that outsourcing the accounting and bookkeeping of a business can have positive impacts including minimizing costs, increasing the correctness and accuracy of numbers to protect businesses from fines, providing for tax optimization, and providing professional advice for the business owners (Fomina & Kolomiiets, 2022). In the study, 18 out of the 22 participants used one or more of these resources The reasons for using a financial professional included an ease on the microentrpreneurs for tax preparations, as this has been deemed nonessential to know the complexities of yearend taxes. Four participants outsourced at the end of the year, and 14 founnd it was best to outsource financial record keeping to professionals, as it leaves them more time to focus on their craft. There were two participants who stated they did not use an external resource for anything because they did all of their financials themselves. Another two participants made no mention of using a financial professional resource, and one participant did not outsource the financials because she is a tax professional and performs the financials for her business, although, she would like to change this.

For other sources of financial information, the participants used the internet to conduct Google and online searches, joined networking groups, and watched videos to further their knowledge in finance (15 out of 22), and 13 of the participants used family and friends for advice and support and 8 participants using other business owners. Shmailan (2016) pointed out that women and men entrepreneurs have different styles of networking; men have larger networks and women have smaller networks. There were no mentions of how big or small the networks of the participants were in this study. Regardless of size, participants in this study conducted networking through various forms, and research indicated that networking has been found to be beneficial to entrepreneurship as networking can help to build relationships to acquire resources in the form of funding, skills, and business services (Redd & Wu, 2020). The importance of networking is also emphasized by I. Liu (2023) as reported in the Milken Institute's 27th Annual Global Conference, indicating that networks are vital to women entrepreneurs as they can provide mentorship and guidance to a company founder.

Theme 3 also is associated with RQ2, in that it revealed that forecasting, a traditional tool used in business (Mamabola & Myres, 2020) was not used by the participants in the study. This theme was mentioned in RQ1; however, it also is related to RQ2, because this was a skill that had been found to not be of importance to the particpants in the study. Nineteen out of the 22 participants did not conduct formal forecasting methods such as straight-line, moving average, simple linear regression, and multiple linear regression to project numbers. The reason for not forecasting was due to unpredictability. Additionally, 5 participants mentioned that it was the least important financial skill, and an additional 5 indicated that they could not forecast due to external factors (e.g., weather, inflation, the economy). Eleven of the 19 participants did conduct variability analysis for forecasting, which is the practice of looking back at previous data points to arrive at averages to predict future earnings (Scott, 2020). The three participants that did look

forward financially do so because one participant just changed her business

model into a cost-sharing operation and as a group, they project as far out as

2 years. The other two participants look forward financially because they

have contracts that are longterm. This was by no means an indication that

participants were missing out on opportunities, as research has indicated that

financial forecasting has been linked to making poor decisions, as it sets a

reference point for the business owner, and when that reference point is not

met, it leads to riskier decision making (Shrader et al., 2021).

In summary, although many of the participants do not participate in

formal financial training due to time, cost, and value, Theme 2 revealed that

they did seek information from external resources such as fintech tools,

financial professionals, networking, family, friends, the internet, and through

reading, which enhances their knowledge in making financial decisions,

which is working for the participants in this study. Another theme that relates

to RQ2 is Theme 5, which is the belief that finance is an intimidating subject

for the participants of this study. This was another reason why they moved

away from formal financial training, as they had all been in business for over

5 years and had managed to survive through the COVID-19 pandemic.

Theme 3 revealed that formal financial forecasting was not used by the

participants of this study, which can be to their benefit because forecasting

has been linked to poor decision making when forecasting goals are not met

(Shrader et al., 2021).

Research Question 3

Figure 5.4 is a visual representation of how the results of the study addressed the third RQ about approaches, strategies, and challenges faced by women microentrepreneurs with the themes that aligned with the RQ. RQ3 of the study was: "What are the financial approaches, strategies, and challenges, if any, faced by women entrepreneurs?"

Figure 5.4

Research Question 3 and Themes

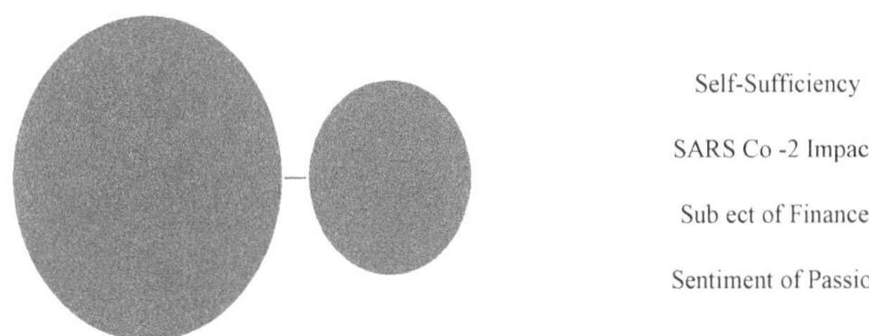

There were four themes from the data analysis that contributed toward answering RQ3 as detailed in Figure 5.4. This section is divided into three sections that include the approaches, strategies, and challenges that the participants faced and were revealed through the four themes.

Approaches

Theme 6 revealed the findings that the main approach that participants had in common was the characteristic of passion, which resonated in every interview that was conducted. Although passion is not a financial skill, as indicated in book, it has been correlated to entrepreneurial performance and considered essential to entrepreneurship and can lead to successful ventures (Cardon et al., 2009; Hu et al., 2022). All participants expressed some form of passion, whether it was their business being their *happy place,* finding it *rewarding,* and having enough passion to enter the world of entrepreneurship.

Another approach that was revealed through Theme 1 was not paying attention to what the competition is doing. According to the Small Business Administration (SBA, 2024), competitiveness is a way for small businesses to gain an advantage over others in the same industry. However, 20 out of 22 participants in this study indicated that paying attention to the competition was a waste of time and rather than competing with others, they looked to other successful business owners in the same industry, realized the uniqueness their business brought to market, and competed with themselves to drive the business. Collaboration over competition was supported by qualitative research conducted by Johnson and Mehta (2024). An exemplary addition to these results was found in one of the participants of this study who recently changed their entire structure to a cost-sharing operation with others in the same industry and at the same location. There were two participants that made no mention of collaborating with the competition, and they did not indicate that competition was something they focused on.

Strategies

Contrary to most of the past research examined in the book review in Chapter 2 that microentrepreneurs are the most vulnerable to financial

instability from crisis events, such as the COVID-19 pandemic (S. Liu &
Parilla, 2020; Miklian & Hoelscher, 2022; Prosperity Now, 2020), Theme 4
found that 19 out of 22 participants saw positive impacts from the pandemic.
This was consistent with Manolova et al.'s (2020) findings that women
entrepreneurs were able to pivot their business models when the pandemic
impacted the world by offering new products and services, transitioning to
online, making accommodations to deliver their products despite shutdowns,
or having enough savings to get through the shutdown period.

Some of the participants included the benefits were monetary in that
they saw increases in revenue and growth, due to the industry they were in,
whereby some were considered essential businesses and others saw an
increase in demand for the products or services during the COVID-19
pandemic. Monetary benefits were indicated by 11 out of the 19 participants.
Eight out of the 19 participants realized benefits that were not monetary.
Rather, the nonmonetary benefits included having the time to take a mental
health break, care for family members, and be a support mechanism for their
communities. The results of the study indicated that personality played an
essential role regarding business outcomes and psychological well-being.
Those who had a positive experience during the pandemic included
personality traits of optimism, openness, motivation, resilience, and an
inclination toward taking risks, which directly goes against the findings of
Shmailan's (2016) characteristic differences between men and women
entrepreneurs of women being risk averse. There was one participant that

indicated the pandemic completely changed her business for the worse, and another two participants made no mention of the pandemic.

Theme 1 was self-sufficiency. Participants who knew and monitored the financial numbers of their business have enabled several participants to create financial strategies on pricing, taxes, and savings, providing them with the ability to analyze their costs, expenses, and worth, and as a result raise prices. A total of 64% (14 out of 22) of the participants indicated that keeping an eye on business numbers have enabled them to evaluate their business and amend their pricing structure to either focus on the segment that offers them more opportunities and recognized the value of their own time by incorporating their labor into their pricing strategies.

Another practice used by participants was to know their numbers well enough to set aside savings. One of the core components, according to the Organization for Economic Cooperation and Development (2023) and the *Big Five* financial literacy assessment (Global Financial Literary Excellence Center, n.d.) used worldwide is saving, and many of the participants followed this basic tenet of financial literacy. Sixteen out of the 22 participants have a savings account and the reason for having savings varies between two categories: (a) saving for unexpected expenses and (b) saving specifically for taxes. Fourteen participants indicated they had a savings account for taxes, and 50% used a process of taking a percentage of each sale to put aside for taxes. A qualitative study by Daher et al. (2022) supported saving on one's own over microcredit programs, as it facilitates women's empowerment and has a significant impact on their psychosocial well-being. Daher et al. added that having savings heightened financial inclusion without having to go into debt. Therefore saving on their own can be viewed as a positive benefit, rather than going through formal channels offered to microenterprises.

Challenges

Theme 4 indicated a challenge that was faced by all of humanity, including economic, social, environmental, educational, and health setbacks (Miyah et al., 2022), which was the COVID-19 pandemic, and the participants in this study were not immune to these challenges. All participants indicated negative impacts during the pandemic, due to mandatory shutdowns and going without an income for the duration of shutdowns. There were a variety of sentiments expressed by the participants that made it a challenging time including "crazy," "challenging," "stressful," "struggle," "hard," and

"rough."

Another challenge faced by the participants was revealed in Theme 5, which indicated the topic of finance is intimidating. This finding resulted in the women interviewed finding very little value in formal financial training courses. Another finding that came out of Theme 5 was that an overwhelming 19 out of 22 participants indicated the negative perception of formal finance training was due to the awareness of the gender disparity that exists between men and women in entrepreneurship. Furthermore, 13 of the 19 participants indicated the gender disparity has harmed their business. Ahl and Marlow (2021) found the most common reason for gender disparity having an impact on business is due to the societal beliefs that portray women as inferior to men, of women being more nurturing, emotional, and empathetic, whereby the masculine discourse in entrepreneurship is taken for granted as being normative. Two participants made no indication of a gender disparity having an impact on their business.

In summary, when it comes to approaches, strategies, and challenges, the participants expressed two approaches that were important to their business, which was indicated through Themes 6 and 1. Having a passion for what they did was found to be an approach used by all participants, which can lead to better financial outcomes. Additionally, Theme 1 indicated another approach used by the participants was not paying attention to what the competition was doing; rather, a better approach was to work with the competition to learn from them. Strategies were identified in Themes 4 and 1, which identified the participants used a variety of strategies to remain operational through the COVID-19 pandemic, whether it was from creating new products, pivoting their businesses online, or using it as a time to take a mental break and strengthen relationships with the community. Theme 1 identified two strategies that resulted from knowing the numbers of their business and monitoring them regularly, which included pricing strategies and a savings strategy. Finally, Themes 4 and 5 identified two challenges faced by the participants, including the pandemic, in which all of humanity faced a challenge, and Theme 5 identified the language of finance was a challenge, which has been found to be intimidating and it has an impact on participating in formal financial courses. Participants also faced challenges

due to the gender gap in finance that has been acknowledged by the

participants. This concludes the section of findings and conclusions of the

research questions. The next section focuses on how the findings can be

applied to the problem statement of the study.

Application of Findings and Conclusions to the Problem Statement

Entrepreneurship has been on the rise in the U.S. and one of the most

important contributing factors to success is financial literacy (Burchi et al.,

2021; Nitani et al., 2020), and microentrepreneurs make up a substantial

portion of small businesses at 92% according to the Association for

Enterprise Opportunity (AEO, 2013). Therefore, listening to the needs of this

demographic of entrepreneurs is vital to economic growth in the U.S. The

general problem is that women in the U.S. have been considered less

financially literate based on quantitative results, which have caused

inequalities in entrepreneurship such as external access to funding, loan

disapprovals, and survival rates. If the gender gaps were closed, it could

result in a 3% to 6% growth in gross domestic product in the U.S. (U.S.

Senate Committee on Small Business & Entrepreneurship, 2023).

Specifically, there is a lack of financial literacy programs for women

microentrepreneurs, which may result in limited knowledge and

understanding of financial skills used and how those skills are obtained, and

the results of this study have confirmed this finding, with only 5 out of 22

participants seeking assistance from nonprofit organizations. The lack of financial literacy programs is for a variety of reasons including the time it takes to complete a course, the cost, determining whether a course may bring any value to microenterprises, and the language that is used in such courses. Therefore, it is recommended that academics, nonprofit organizations, government entities, and private organizations pay attention to the needs of this quickly growing segment of entrepreneurs in the Pacific Northwest. As a result of the findings from the study, the following actions can be implemented.

At a minimum, policymakers, government entities, nonprofit organizations, and private organizations in the Pacific Northwest should consider developing a collaborative definition of a microentrepreneur. In 2013, AEO referred to microentrepreneurs as a business with less than 5 employees, and in 2024 the AEO referred to microenterprises as a business with 0 to 9 employees. In doing so, results on gaps could worsen, or become narrower. According to AEO (2024), under their new definition of a microenterprise (0 to 9 employees), this demographic makes up 96% of all small businesses. However, according to the Washington State Microenterprise Association (n.d.), their definition of a microenterprise is one to 5 employees, including the business owner. Consistency in measuring all aspects of microenterprises can have huge impacts on this demographic and could result in appropriate funding remedies and training needs. Beginning with the states in the Pacific Northwest should be a start to a collaborative definition so that statistical reporting is more accurate, which can lend itself to critical data that can be used throughout the U.S.

Policymakers in the Pacific Northwest should consider the changing needs of entrepreneurship in the 21st century to better understand their needs and recognize that this segment contributes to one quarter of the U.S. workforce (AEO, 2024), and efforts should be made to continue this optimistic trend. This could be in the form of policies on self-employment by creating a new tax structure for microenterprises, offering grants to microenterprises, and developing affordable health benefits and retirement programs.

The gender gap in earnings among microentrepreneurs also needs to be addressed, as indicated in Chapter 2. The AEO (2013) reported on the statistics of microenterprises and the gap widens as there are more earnings. The number of microentrepreneurs that dedicate 100% of their time to their venture and earn $50,000 or more is 61% of men, versus 18% of women. Focusing on microenterprises in the Pacific Northwest can yield results that could potentially highlight geographical locations where the gender gaps in earnings are prevalent and can add valuable information to research.

Academia, including high schools, institutions of higher education, professors, and researchers in the Pacific Northwest can act by using the results of this research to create programs that are industry specific and focus on various dimensions of entrepreneurship instead of placing entrepreneurship under one umbrella. For example, there should be different programs and courses that are developed that cater to future entrepreneurs who wish to become a unicorn and those who wish to remain small and operate with 0 to 4 employees. Each looks at business very differently and having different programs and courses can help aspiring entrepreneurs on a path to success.

Therefore, recognition of the differences in new business ventures should be identified to be able to offer services that cater to microentrepreneurs, which can address the lack in programs that exist for this specific demographic.

The findings of the study indicated that women microenterprises were aware of the gender gaps, but they also have partaken in many techniques to remain self-sufficient. However, many feel the topic of finance is intimidating, which was one of the reasons they did not pursue additional formal financial training. Therefore, policymakers and academia in the Pacific Northwest should take into consideration the language that is used by the growing segment of microentrepreneurs and explore updating books, courses, and laws that are familiar to microentrepreneurs. Rather than using formal channels to increase their financial skills, participants turned to various other resources to enhance their financial knowledge, with only a small number using nonprofit organizational support, which supports the specific problem of the study. Closing the language gap in finance could help to diminish feelings of intimidation and gain more traction in formal training for microentrepreneurs in the Pacific Northwest, and if the results indicated microentrepreneurs are frequenting external support to increase their financial

literacy skills, this could be rolled out across the nation.

The results of the study also identified techniques that were not

essential to microenterprises such as forecasting and paying attention to the

competition. Therefore, policymakers and academics in the Pacific Northwest

should take this information into consideration and develop more ways for

microenterprises to collaborate with one another, because they find it

extremely helpful. For forecasting, again, there is book that discusses the

various forms of forecasting, such as straight-line, moving average, simple

linear regression, and multiple linear regression (Boyles, 2022). Rather than

using the financial nomenclature, which is foreign to the microenterprises

interviewed, there should be more investigation into whether

microenterprises are missing out on an opportunity by not forecasting or if

setting goals and looking backwards is the norm for this demographic.

Another action that can be implemented is highlighting passion and

resilience, which were findings in the study. All participants interviewed

survived through the COVID-19 pandemic due to several reasons, which is

an indication of resilience, and each displayed a passion for what they do.

Therefore, programs can be developed in the Pacific Northwest that focus on

specific industries of entrepreneurship, which could yield better results of

resiliency.

Action can be taken by existing microenterprises by sharing the results

of this research with other and future women entrepreneurs to better

understand that they are not alone in their ways of running a business and
their confidence, self-efficacy, and resilience should not be seen as
detriments; rather, they should be celebrated as characteristics that are
helping to close the gender gap in entrepreneurship. This could result in a
boost in confidence, which is strongly related to more profitable ventures as
indicated in book.

Application to Business

Throughout history, entrepreneurship has been the backbone of
democracy, to reduce poverty, create jobs, and ignite the economy (Lee &
Rodriguez-Pos, 2020). Women entrepreneurs have affected economic growth
in the U.S., contributing $1.8 trillion to the economy and employing over 10
million workers in 2019 (SBA, 2023b).

The SBA reported that women entrepreneurs have impacted economic
growth in the U.S.
The economic conditions continued to improve in the U.S. into 2021, with
$3.0 trillion in sales, representing 23 million workers (World Bank, n.d.).
Applying the findings of the study can help to boost economic growth and the
themes that were derived from the data analysis for microenterprises in the
Pacific Northwest can be applied to business to close the gender gap in
entrepreneurship and financial literacy in the following manners:

(a) Training programs and/or business forms supplied to

microenterprises in the Pacific Northwest could explore adopting a

language that is comfortable to those that are in more creative

fields, as some of the microentrepreneurs have never taken a business class. Language that is used is intimidating to them. One of the participants indicated that she took advantage of a course that was taught on how to fill out the forms for a PPP loan, which was time consuming. The language that is used has deterred women microentrepreneurs in this study from furthering their financial skills, and because this segment of entrepreneurs is growing rapidly, using nomenclature that is not foreign could aid with the survival rates of women microenterprises in the Pacific Northwest.

(b) Website developers that produce local financial training for microenterprises in the Pacific Northwest at the county level can consider looking at ways of making tutorials and/or formal online training classes easier to find. This can be done by using tags in their website pages and using the terminology that is familiar to microenterprises instead of using financial nomenclature.

(c) Fintech developers could explore tools that are more affordable for microenterprises, who may not need all the bells and whistles that come with some tools. Furthermore, accounting software tools, such as QuickBooks and FreshBooks can consider incorporating artificial intelligence into their software and prepare a skill assessment for potential customers on accounting. In doing so, manufacturers of the software can identify areas where additional training may be required by the user and the user can then assess

the time commitment that may be required to use the software
effectively. Because time has been found to be a factor for
microentrepreneurs, having an idea of the time required to learn
accounting software can help to better prepare users to set aside a
schedule to increase their financial literacy skills.

(d) Entrepreneurial and/or business courses offered by corporations,
such as Goldman Sachs 10,000 Women initiative could explore
using a quantitative form that must be filled out prior to someone
signing up for a course. This can be rolled out to microenterprises
in the Pacific Northwest as a trial. The results of the quantitative
data can then use artificial intelligence to create trainings that are
beneficial for individuals' needs. Should it be found that
developing courses based off user input increases participation,
consideration should be made to introduce specific trainings in
other geographical locations.

(e) Nano learning and microlearning trainings could be useful training
methodologies that can be adopted for financial training for
microentrepreneurs in the Pacific Northwest to provide quick
access to shorter material on a particular subject, which can aid in
decision making. Using these forms of training for
microentrepreneurs, instead of e-learning modules that
are much longer in duration, can help mitigate the issue of time to
learn new financial skills.

In summary, there are steps that can be taken by businesses, academia, and nonprofit institutions to introduce different learning techniques into their services or curriculum through nano and micro learning. These are shorter modules that cater to a specific need. Women and other microentrepreneurs can benefit from these types of courses because of the time duration required, which is less than the typically ecommerce courses being offered. Additionally, if corporations and nonprofit institutions wish to continue the modular way of offering courses, they could take into consideration the language that is used for such programs are written in a language that is familiar to microentrepreneurs, as indicated in this study. Curriculum development could follow the same premise of offering courses that use nomenclature that is familiar to microenterprises. Corporations should also take into consideration the services they are selling and to whom. Although QuickBooks and other fintech accounting software offer a great solution to easier management of bookkeeping services, these companies should pay more attention to their audience's needs and provide pretesting prior to purchasing to ensure they can accommodate future clients. All these actions can benefit microentrepreneurs by saving time, cutting costs, and ensuring they are being served with the appropriate needs for their businesses.

Recommendations for Action

Based on the results of the study, many of the participants do not seek financial support from nonprofit organizations due to time, cost, value, and intimidation. The first recommendation for action is to place more recognition on microentrepreneurs that have less than 5 employees because

their situations are unique in that many are solopreneurs and they do not see

the value of taking a financial course that is designed for a business that is

larger. Therefore, the following recommendations to increase financial

literacy skills of women microenterprises are as follows:

(a) Institute nano and micro learning techniques into entrepreneurial

training for financial literacy to women microenterprises in the

Pacific Northwest. Nano and micro learning videos provide shorter

segments of education on specific topics, which can increase the

knowledge of microentrepreneurs. Both forms of training have been

found to have benefits in saving time. First, learning specific skills

in increments has been found to increase the efficiency of learning,

and through repetition, microlearning can contribute to knowledge

building, by taking short-term memory and transferring it into long-

term memory (Aburizaizah & Albaiz, 2021). If the results prove to

be beneficial, these types of trainings can be rolled out across the

nation or in increments, geographically.

(b) When creating any type of a financial program for microenterprises

in the Pacific Northwest, whether it is an online course through a

government entity, corporation, or academia, the language that is

used should be written to include familiar financial terms of

microenterprises instead of using financial jargon to lessen the

burden of learning a new language, which was determined to be one of the reasons why microenterprises cannot gain access to finance

(Sawhney, 2022).

(c) Develop a comprehensive and collaborative definition of what a microenterprise is in the Pacific Northwest to be able to cater to this demographic and report on them in a uniformed manner so that courses and curriculums can be developed to accommodate their specific needs. In doing so, the findings can lend itself to determining the true number of microenterprises in the Pacific Northwest and can determine if their needs are being met.

(d) To become an entrepreneur in a digitalized world has made entry much easier. The advent of social media tools such as Etsy, Pinterest, Tik Tok, and Amazon Market Place have made it much easier to enter the market. Therefore, microentrepreneurs could use tools created to teach the skills necessary to adapt to having an online presence, including a cost-analysis on which platform would be best, based on entrepreneurial aspirations to increase the longevity of microentrepreneurs.

(e) Ensure that the fintech tools that are being offered are affordable and address the needs of microentrepreneurs through preselling techniques that protect an investment by the microentrepreneur.

(f) Introduce a quantitative financial literacy test to microenterprises in the Pacific Northwest that uses the language familiar to microenterprises to determine if there is a financial literacy gap among this demographic in this geographical location. The findings could result in narrowing the gap of financial literacy between men and women in the Pacific Northwest.

In summary, the findings of this study indicated two major hurdles to acquiring financial skills: (a) time and (b) language. Therefore, the recommendations previously mentioned could provide solutions for microentrepreneurs to continuously work at their craft and improve their financial skills to hopefully close the gender gap in financial literacy.

Recommendations for Further Research

Much was learned about the specific demographic of women microentrepreneurs; however, there is still an abundance of additional research that should be conducted to add to the book of this group. The further research is broken down into five topics.

- Develop a quantitative tool that is geared toward microenterprises, instead of using the questions that are used by the *Big Five* (Fisher & Ryan, 2021;

Lusardi & Mitchell, 2014; Milken Institute, 2021; U.S. Financial Literacy and Education Commission, 2020; World Bank, n.d.), and the FINRA Investor Education Foundation (Urban & Valdes 2022), which are geared toward readiness for retirement and places women at a disadvantage because they perform lower than men. In doing so, questions should be geared toward finding out the needs of microenterprises, which could have an impact on the gender gap in financial literacy, and it can provide women microentrepreneurs with more confidence around financial matters.

- Another area for future research is to conduct a similar study on the male demographic of microentrepreneurs to see if the findings of this study are similar or different. As an example, would the results indicate that passion is a driving force for men microentrepreneurs as it is for the women in this study?

- There should be more similar studies conducted on entrepreneurship, using a qualitative methodology, which is broader in scope, to include entrepreneurs with more than 5 employees to see if the findings are similar or different, which could substantiate the need for specialized training for microenterprises.

- Further research should focus on microenterprises in different geographical locations in the U.S. and focus on the same number of employees, whether it is 0 or less than 5 employees, to see if the findings are similar or different. The results of such a study could determine if geographical location has an impact on access to financial literacy resources.

- Finally, there should be more research on the gender disparity in entrepreneurship and financial literacy for microenterprises to see if there are additional findings that could potentially help to close the gap. For example, the most cited gender gap in entrepreneurship is gaining access to financing and running out of cash to continue business operations (Safari & Das, 2023). However, the participants from the study did not exclusively state this as being a problem for them. Rather, the results of the study indicated the gender disparity is due to distinct factors such as societal factors, stereotyping, the language of finance, and intimidation.

Concluding Statement

This phenomenological qualitative research study focused on women entrepreneurs and financial literacy to better understand the financial literacy gap between men and women through the lens of poststructural feminist theory, which resulted in different perspectives of what constitutes a deficiency in financial literacy skills of women entrepreneurs versus what is essential for them to know. A total of 22 interviews were conducted with women microenterprises in the Pacific Northwest, representing 13 counties across Idaho, Montana, Oregon, and Washington states, representing more than 50% of North American Industry Classification System code industries. Each participant was considered a microentrepreneur, in which all the businesses had 0 to 4 employees. There were also date parameters set for an active business, which was inception before 2019 through March 14, 2020 (before), March 15,

2020, through May 31, 2021 (during) and June 1, 2021, and thereafter (post-COVID-19). The focus on microentrepreneurs was a deliberate attempt to find out if the gender gaps in entrepreneurship and financial literacy were applicable to this specific demographic, because the government has recognized the gaps in entrepreneurship through the Women Entrepreneur's initiative, which aims at increasing women's participation in entrepreneurship to bolster the economy (USPTO, 2022).

The following section summarizes the three research questions that were used to contribute to existing book on the gender disparity in entrepreneurship and financial literacy. The section contains any surprising or interesting findings, followed by the concluding statement.

RQ1 identified women entrepreneurs' perceptions of the impact on their business through the lens of their current financial literacy and revealed that knowing the numbers of their business was vital to their continuation. To help them remain self-sufficient, they saved for taxes or the unexpected, and they priced their services and products to ensure their labor was accounted for.

RQ2 identified how women entrepreneurs acquired the financial skills that were used in their business, which resulted in a small number of participants using formal channels to acquire additional financial skills because time, money, and value of formal courses was a hurdle that many opted not to focus on. However, most of the participants gained financial knowledge through informal channels, including family and friends, the internet, financial professionals, and using fintech tools to help streamline business operations.

RQ3 identified financial approaches, strategies, and challenges that are faced by women entrepreneurs and resulted in the surprising findings of two common strategies touted in business as useful that are not used by microentrepreneurs, which were forecasting and competition. Additionally, many of the participants were aware of the gender gaps in financial literacy, and this has contributed to the challenge of acquiring additional skills because of the financial nomenclature used in formal trainings, making it intimidating to the participants. Another challenge for the microentrepreneurs interviewed was the COVID-19 pandemic, which was not surprising; however, the findings that most experienced positive impacts from the pandemic were a bit surprising. The most surprising finding on approaches to conducting their businesses was the passion that every participant experienced.

Although the research intended to explore the financial literacy skills of women entrepreneurs, emphasizing the gender gap in access to finance, the results of the study did not result in information on borrowing and lending practices of the participants. Rather, the microenterprises that were interviewed recognized a gender gap in entrepreneurship in other areas such as the financial nomenclature that is used in business
and they have employed approaches, strategies, and mindsets to set themselves up for success.

In conclusion, the findings from this study have revealed what is important and not important for women microentrepreneurs. Gender disparity in financial literacy is a known factor for women. However, despite the challenges faced by the women microenterprises interviewed, all managed to sustain their business through the COVID19 pandemic and continued to operate tenable businesses. Action needs to be taken to close the gender gaps in entrepreneurship and financial literacy and the findings from this study can be a starting point for the specific demographic of microentrepreneurs. Financial literacy scores may improve; however, if there was a specific financial literacy assessment for microentrepreneurs that used the language that they use in their world, it may result in measuring the real level of financial literacy for this group and could result in finding that women microentrepreneurs are financially literate.